"What a fun read! This adorable, thorough guide leaves no dish un-turned. It's ideal for first-time parents, or for the seasoned mom or dad who finds themselves with a challenging eater. It's also a great reminder that modeling great food habits is an important ⬚⬚⬚⬚ ⬚⬚ ⬚⬚⬚⬚⬚⬚⬚⬚"

—Abigail Tuller, editor-at⬚⬚⬚⬚ ⬚⬚⬚⬚⬚⬚ ⬚⬚⬚⬚⬚ ⬚⬚⬚⬚⬚⬚⬚

"Mealtime with infants doesn't have to be stressful! Melanie Potock an⬚ ⬚⬚⬚⬚⬚⬚⬚ ⬚⬚⬚⬚⬚⬚ created a premier resource to educate and empower parents to confi⬚⬚ ⬚⬚⬚⬚⬚⬚⬚⬚⬚⬚ about their child's first experiences with food. Here's to more happy, healthy eaters and their proud parents!"

—Jena Castro-Casbon, M.S., CCC-SLP, founder of The Independent Clinician

"Figuring out when and how to introduce your baby to solid foods can be confusing. This must-read guide helps you find a perfect balance between traditional purees and finger foods to get your baby started right. This stress-free plan for beginning solids can set your child up for a happy, healthy, and adventurous life-long relationship with food, and can prevent many of the picky-eating problems that crop up during those early years."

—Elizabeth Pantley, author of The *No-Cry Picky Eater Solution*

"*Baby Self-Feeding* provides parents with easy-to-read essential guidance to help your baby happily navigate the road to self-feeding. It includes sound practical advice about balancing nutrition, your infant's preferences, and confidently supporting independence and eating skills. Based on science but balanced with down-to-earth tips on how to best feed your baby, this wonderful contribution to infant feeding is sure to be highly recommended by both feeding specialists and pediatricians."

—Catherine S. Shaker, M.S., CCC-SLP, BCS-S, pediatric speech-language pathologist and infant feeding/swallowing specialist

"Research shows that babies greatly benefit from a variety of feeding experiences beginning at 6 months of age. Spoon feeding, open cup drinking, straw drinking, and finger feeding provide the mouth movement and development that babies need. Using a program that promotes variety in feeding methods, such as Baby Self-Feeding, guides parents through these crucial feeding processes."

—Diane Bahr, M.S., CCC-SLP, author of *Nobody Ever Told Me (or My Mother) That! Everything from Bottles and Breathing to Healthy Speech Development*

"*Baby Self-Feeding* celebrates the partnership between baby and parent as baby learns to love food and participate joyfully in mealtimes while becoming an independent eater!"

—Marsha Dunn Klein, M.Ed., OTR/L, FAOTA

BABY SELF-FEEDING

SOLID FOOD SOLUTIONS TO CREATE LIFELONG, HEALTHY EATING HABITS

NANCY RIPTON &
MELANIE POTOCK M.A., CCC-SLP, CO-AUTHOR OF
RAISING A HEALTHY, HAPPY EATER

FAIR WINDS

Quarto is the authority on a wide range of topics.

Quarto educates, entertains and enriches the lives of our readers—enthusiasts and lovers of hands-on living.

www.QuartoKnows.com

First published in the United States of America in 2016 by
Fair Winds Press, an imprint of
Quarto Publishing Group USA Inc.
100 Cummings Center
Suite 406-L
Beverly, Massachusetts 01915-6101
Telephone: (978) 282-9590
Fax: (978) 283-2742
QuartoKnows.com
Visit our blogs at QuartoKnows.com

20 19 18 17 16   1 2 3 4 5

ISBN: 978-1-59233-722-4

Digital edition published in 2016
eISBN: 978-1-63159-167-9

Library of Congress Cataloging-in-Publication Data

Names: Ripton, Nancy, author. | Potock, Melanie, author.
Title: Baby self-feeding : solid food solutions to create lifelong, healthy
   eating habits / Nancy Ripton and Melanie Potock.
Description: Beverly, Massachusetts : Quarto Publishing Group, USA, Inc.,
   2016] | Includes bibliographical references and index.
Identifiers: LCCN 2016004084| ISBN 9781592337224 (softbound) | ISBN
   9781631591679 (eISBN)
Subjects: LCSH: Infants--Nutrition. | Baby foods.
Classification: LCC RJ216 .R552 2016 | DDC 641.3/00832--dc23
LC record available at http://lccn.loc.gov/2016004084

Design and Page Layout: Mattie Wells

Photography & Cover Image: Glenn Scott Photography

Additional Photography: Shutterstock.com pages 12, 14, 38, 44, 57, 64, 78, 92, 106, 130, 136, 142, 146, and 150; Alamy.com page 192.

Printed in China

The information in this book is for educational purposes only. It is not intended to replace the advice of a physician or medical practitioner. Please see your health care provider before beginning any new health program. Speak with your health care provider if you suspect your child may have a food allergy. Do not leave children unattended while eating.

Contents

- INTRODUCTION -
Creating Healthy Eaters for Life

The first year of parenting is an overwhelming and rewarding time. The feeling of being responsible for the health and safety of a brand-new human being is frightening, yet empowering. Where do we start? With the basics—sleep, first feedings, and lots of love.

The nutrients a healthy baby will receive for those first months of life will come from the breast or bottle. However, once it is time for your infant to explore the world of solid foods, things become more complex. This book will assist you in making proper feeding choices that are tailored to your baby's development and tastes. A sound nutritional basis will empower your child to make healthy food choices and embrace adventurous eating.

Looking back over the past century, the way in which we feed our babies has changed dramatically. Methods popular in the past have often reflected fear and cultural trends rather than proper research, or they focused on extreme or strict rules rather than trusting parents' judgment. These days we have unparalleled access to facts, options, and historical data in regard to infant nutrition. But this book is not about promoting a specific diet. It's a tool to help you make the best choices for your baby—and to help you empower your child to make those choices in the future.

Baby Self-Feeding responds directly to some strict trends. On one end of the spectrum are parents who feed their babies exclusively purees for a prolonged period of time— up to a year and beyond. They may choose to make all their food at home with organic fruits and vegetables and free-range meats, or they may opt for store-bought varieties (often organic). Puree-based diets are based on research that fruits and veggies are healthy; however, too much of a good thing can backfire developmentally. Many parents feed purees much longer than necessary, thereby pushing back on a key developmental period, often because they are fearful of choking or because they don't trust their baby has the necessary skills yet.

At the other extreme are parents who shun purees entirely, opting to feed baby the same food everyone else is eating from day one of feeding. These proponents of baby-led weaning (BLW) begin solid foods from about six months of age. Strict BLW adherents argue that purees are unnecessary and avoid them entirely. The theory behind BLW, and it's one we agree with, is that letting your child feed himself will give him a developmental boost and make for smarter, more engaged children who are better able to self-regulate their food intake both now and later in life. But, as this book will examine, research shows that purees are also beneficial and help some babies properly transition from breast milk to solid food.

Finding Balance

You don't need to choose between handheld foods and purees. Both play a role in your child's early mouth development and her taste preferences. As feeding specialist Diane Bahr, M.S., CCC-SLP, said, "Children need to have experiences with all types of textures."

Both camps agree on the importance of early child nutrition. The first year or two of life is a time of high plasticity. During this time your child will undergo dramatic transitions in the ways he ingests food. It's a time of prime nutritional programming where the taste preferences he develops can last a lifetime. These food choices also impact development, health, ability to self-regulate food, and the risk of obesity later in life.

Good nutrition is a balancing act, and this book is not intended as a set of strict guidelines. Review nutritional information we present in the following pages and weigh advantages of these tips and techniques to determine what's best for your baby and for your family.

We encourage you to make your own informed decision on whether or not to feed purees. Like finger foods, purees play an important role in mouth development and learning to accept different food tastes and textures. In our view, purees should be a part of your child's early food experience and beyond, in conjunction with safe finger foods or handheld foods. Young children can handle different tastes, textures, and feeding experiences. Sampling a variety of foods now leads to a child who is a more adventurous eater later in life.

> A SOUND NUTRITIONAL BASIS WILL EMPOWER YOUR CHILD TO MAKE HEALTHY FOOD CHOICES AND EMBRACE ADVENTUROUS EATING.

While parents have to be aware of safety, babies tend to be much more capable than we give them credit for. Be aware of choking risks and potential allergens, so that you can take the necessary precautions and be able to safely offer developmentally appropriate food for your child to enjoy. If you're unsure of where to start, we've provided a list of recipes in chapters 10, 11, and 12 that are suitable for a variety of ages starting at about 6 months.

This book is about sorting through the facts and offering a balanced approach to early nutrition that takes away the fear of early feeding. By offering current studies, research, and social implications of different feeding techniques, we aim to take the guesswork out of how to best feed your baby. Our ultimate goal is to provide your baby with all the crucial nutrients she needs to thrive, produce optimal developmental results, and set your child up for a lifetime of rewarding food experiences.

CHAPTER 1

The Evolution of Baby Feeding

When we were children, our mothers wouldn't have even thought to cook peaches, throw them in a blender, and make their own baby food. They bought white rice cereal and pureed baby food in little glass jars. Broccoli florets and stewed beef? These weren't even conceivably on the baby menu. The 1950s to late 1970s was the golden age of mass-produced baby food. During this time roughly 90 percent of North American babies were fed store-bought pureed baby food. The convenience made commercial baby food the most popular feeding choice, even though it had not existed thirty years earlier.

The Rise of Pureed Baby Food

During the late 1800s and early 1900s parents avoided feeding their babies food until at least nine months of age, generally feeding babies breast milk alone until their first birthday. "There was a general feeling that it was very dangerous to feed your baby anything other than breast milk," says Amy Bentley, a food historian and associate professor at New York University and author of *Inventing Baby Food*. In the late 1800s there were some liquid formulas, but they were lacking in vitamins and nutrients. They were not always made with clean water or served in sterilized bottles. Babies who drank these formulas often fell ill, which made parents fearful of feeding their baby from a bottle. If women were unable or unwilling to breastfeed their baby for the first year of life, it was common practice to hire a wet nurse to breastfeed the baby in place of the mother.

Starting in the 1940s, it was believed that formula and baby purees were the best choice for early nutrition.

"There was an idea at the time that you shouldn't feed your baby solids until she had teeth to chew with," continues Bentley. "Purees didn't really exist." On occasions when babies were fed food prior to their teeth cutting through, they were fed similar foods to those given to invalids and the elderly. Porridge and beef broths were both popular, as was gruel.

At the turn of the twentieth century, the closest thing to baby puree was gruel, which was made by dripping small amounts of boiling water onto flour and salt until it formed a paste. The paste was then added back to the boiling water and stirred until it formed a semifluid consistency. Finally, it was strained to eliminate the film, cooled, and served to the baby.

Fruits and veggies were to be avoided until babies were at least two years of age. Produce was believed to have a laxative effect. Dysentery and cholera were widespread at the time, and there was a lot of fear and confusion over how these diseases were transmitted. Parents felt that avoiding fruits and veggies in the early years protected their children from extreme illness and possibly even death.

THE FIRST BABY PUREES

In the early 1900s, researchers discovered the presence of vitamins in fruits and veggies. Experts found that including produce in early diets was actually beneficial for health. At the same time came the invention of canning and the industrialization of food.

The food world was also enthralled with the teachings of Horace Fletcher, a turn-of-the century American health food enthusiast nicknamed "The Great Masticator." Fletcher argued that each bite of food should be chewed 32 times before being swallowed. The idea was that food had to basically be pulverized in order to properly mix with saliva and for the body to absorb all the nutritional benefits without taxing the digestive system. It caught on quickly—records show that well-known figures from the Rockefellers to Mark Twain began to chew their foods to a pulp.

During a time when many feared cholera and dysentery, fiber was thought to be a cause of disease. While nutrition experts began encouraging parents to feed fruits and vegetables to babies, they were also very cautious about fiber intake. Fiber must be mitigated in produce. Parents were advised to feed their babies fruits and vegetables, but only if they could break down the cellulose by cooking them down, thus altering the food's natural rough texture.

The texture of the original baby food purees had less to do with the safety of babies' eating the product and more to do with the attempt to eliminate fiber and make the food easier to digest. "There was a belief that the digestive system was not strong enough for rough food," says Bentley. "Professionals, women, and most certainly small children were thought to be especially susceptible to roughage. While the working class could handle more fiber, these more pampered and vulnerable digestive systems could not."

Since babies are unable to fully chew their food, parents were advised to cook food for hours before blending it into a smooth puree, a time-consuming process. When baby food companies such as Gerber and Clapp's emerged in the 1920s, parents were quick to latch on to an easier method for feeding their children. Mass-produced pureed baby food appeared to be nutritious, convenient, and safe.

By the late 1940s, breastfeeding had dropped dramatically as the belief grew that food and formula were effective and adequate. "There was an idea at this time that we could manufacture food that was better than nature," says Bentley. "The U.S. was seen as a super power that was wealthy and driven by science and technology." Feeding your baby scientifically derived formula and baby food was a sign of prestige and power.

This trend continued through to the late '70s and early '80s, when researchers learned the benefits of fiber. Scientists also discovered that adding lots of sugar, salt, and preservatives to baby food was unhealthy. Companies began to make pureed foods as naturally as possible while still preserving their shelf life.

MORE CHOICES IN PUREES

In the past decade, baby food has under gone a health makeover. With research constantly changing, the decisions parents make for feeding their babies have also shifted. It's become clear in recent years that fresh foods are best—not just for baby but also for the entire family. Parents are increasingly making their own purees at home. In fact, the sales of commercially prepared baby food in the United States have been steadily falling since 2005 at a rate of about 4 percent per year (in spite of a baby boom). The sales are dropping just as steadily in Europe.

More prominent now are organic jarred and frozen baby foods that need to be thawed and heated prior to serving. While this extra step isn't always convenient, it does reduce the need for any preservatives and keeps store-bought baby food as natural as possible. Companies such as Sprout Organic Foods produce resealable aluminum packages specially designed to allow optimal freshness and convenience. These products are becoming increasingly popular in an attempt to find a healthy product that is also easy to prepare and serve.

However, even with smaller companies hitting the market, about a third of moms are still choosing to puree their own baby food. While not as time-consuming as it was when baby purees were first introduced—parents no longer need to boil carrots for four hours and then blend them to a pulp—making purees does take a lot of time.

Food in a Pouch

Aluminum pouch squeezable containers are the ultimate in convenience and appeal to older children, thus extending the life of baby food. Despite the decreasing trend of store-bought pureed baby food, parents who are still using mass-produced baby food are using it for longer. Toddlers and even children as old as five or six are still consuming purees from a pouch. While pouch purees are fine for the occasional snack on the go, they can be high in sugar and overuse interferes with learning proper eating techniques. They should be used on special occasions, rather than for everyday fare.

What if there was an easier way? What if you could eliminate or at least reduce the amount of time your baby eats pureed foods? Since pureed baby foods were originally developed as a way to remove fiber, and many solid foods are soft enough for little ones to eat without teeth, we can safely reevaluate this question. We know babies can handle fiber, and that it is good for them. We have been brought up to believe that since babies do not have teeth, and have never eaten any solid food, they cannot handle solids so early. But what if that's not entirely true?

Baby-Led Weaning

About 10 years ago, a British midwife and health visitor (or public health nurse) named Gill Rapley coined the term "baby-led weaning" as an alternative method of introducing first foods to your baby. With baby-led weaning (BLW), parents offer solid foods when babies are six months old. Rapley explains that by this time an infant has the ability to sit up and grasp her own food and can learn to feed herself with finger foods. Rather than being spoon-fed purees by an adult, the baby-led child feeds herself with handheld foods. The baby shares in family mealtimes and is offered the same food as everyone else at the table. Food sizes are small—usually fist size (preferably in the shape of a chip or stick)—so the baby can hold on to and gum it until she learns to chew.

Baby-Led Weaning (BLW) Defined

In the U.K., the word *weaning* means introducing your baby to solid foods, as opposed to the North American meaning of transitioning your baby off breast milk. *Baby-led weaning* means to give your child solid foods and let him feed himself from day one as opposed to spoon feeding your child purees.

The fundamentals of baby-led weaning are as follows: BLW begins around six months of age. Baby must be able to sit up straight and grasp food. Baby shares in mealtimes, often eating the same food as the rest of the family. There are no spoon-fed purees.

Parents should not expect their child to eat all of the food she is offered; often there will be lots leftover. Nor should a child be expected to eat every type of food that is placed in front of her. If your baby doesn't want to eat a particular food, simply take the food away and offer it again at another meal.

Parents are also warned that this type of feeding is messy. Baby-led weaning can be lots of fun and offers quality family time. Just know that mealtimes with baby in charge means food will get everywhere!

The Baby Self-Feeding (BSF) Way

While there are many benefits to early self-feeding, these advantages are not dependent on the shunning of purees. In fact, purees play a vital role in the development of proper mastication techniques. Most early feeding practices focus on one type of eating—only purees, only solids, only introducing one or two new foods a week. Baby self-feeding is about providing your child with the opportunity for a variety of different feeding practices as soon as she is developmentally able to slurp, sip, suck, or chew foods. This variety is essential for proper feeding development and helps create adventurous eaters from an early age.

VARIETY LEADS TO ADVENTUROUS EATERS

There is a time period in which children are more willing and adaptable to try and accept new foods. What you feed your baby from 6 to 12 months can have a lasting impact on the way she will eat and how willing she will be to eat a healthy, varied diet later in life. Research shows that infants who were repeatedly exposed to a variety of solid foods during infancy had a greater acceptance of fruits and vegetables later on in childhood. If children are often fed apples, carrots, and peas as a baby, they are more likely to want those foods later on when they are able to make food choices for themselves.

The problem is that apple puree has none of the texture and very little of the taste of a real apple. The same is true of any puree. Although purees have a developmental role in early feeding, if you feed your child only purees for an extended period of time, you are in essence training him to like sugary, processed, bland, reduced-fiber, ultra-smooth versions of the real thing.

While you have control over the processed and bland components if you make your own purees, you still aren't teaching your child about different tastes and textures. Purees should be just one of the tastes and textures your child experiences. If you focus only on purees for longer than the first month or two of feeding, then you're programing your baby to eat traditional "kid's fare," which is bland, sweet, and easy to swallow, over the healthy foods you would like him to choose once he has mastered the basic techniques of eating. Purees play a role, but they shouldn't be the only food texture your young child experiences.

> "I WANT MY CHILDREN TO KNOW AND UNDERSTAND WHAT THEY'RE EATING FROM THE BEGINNING. THIS STARTS WITH FEEDING THEM REAL, WHOLE FOODS."
>
> —Danielle Fleckenstein, mother of three

BABY SELF-FEEDING CAN REDUCE PICKY EATING

Dr. Amy Brown first became interested in the early introduction of solid foods in 2006, when she was weaning her first child. "Baby-led weaning seemed to have growing interest and popularity, with a book and websites, but I noticed that although there were many anecdotal claims about how baby-led weaning might affect child weight and eating behavior there were no published empirical studies on the approach," says Brown. An associate professor in public health and policy studies at Swansea University in Wales, Brown set out to research the trend of baby-led weaning and see whether it really could impact the way kids viewed food down the road.

One of Brown's most significant studies looked at 423 mothers with infants ages 6 to 12 months who had started to receive their first foods. The mothers completed a questionnaire about their feeding style. Brown followed up with the mothers when their children were between the ages of 18 and 24 months of age to see whether the way in which they were introduced to solids foods impacted their level of fussiness, the way they ate, and their obesity levels a year later. Infants who followed a baby-led weaning style were rated as significantly less fussy than infants who had been spoon-fed purees for an extended time period, both at the initial report when food was being introduced and at the follow-up report a year later.

"I think there are a range of reasons for this," says Brown. For starters, children like to be made a part of the feeding process. While spoon-feeding a 6-month-old has benefits, these benefits quickly diminish with age and can be counterproductive around 8 to 10 months. Kids who are active in the feeding process from an early age learn to monitor their foods and explore new tastes.

"It's also possible that baby-led weaning parents offer a wider range of foods that you wouldn't find in commercial purees, so babies get more exposure to different foods from the beginning," says Brown. The added exposure makes them less picky. The more tastes and textures you can expose your child to from an early age, the better. "All the benefits of the BLW study are still possible with the use of some purees," says Brown. However, purees should only be used exclusively for a limited amount of time and after that should be one part of a larger feeding pattern.

Studies have found that we learn to prefer what becomes familiar. Observational learning also impacts a child's food intake. Since baby self-feeding involves having the child at the table with the family and eating many of the same foods as everyone else, she is learning to accept the same foods as her parents eat from day one. Provided that parents are making healthy food choices for themselves, it makes sense that babies who watch their parents eat and are continually offered similar foods turn into kids who will take part in the family meal and not ask for different foods.

If you offer your baby only purees for too long, it may be more difficult to transition her to new foods. It's a big leap to expect your child to suddenly start eating the same foods as you eat. If, however, you gradually introduce solids from the beginning, your child will learn to expect to eat the same food everyone else at the family table is eating.

PROLONGED, EXCLUSIVE PUREES CREATE A PREFERENCE FOR SWEETER FOODS

As parents we are continually reminded not to feed our babies fruit juice. If we do, it's highly recommended that we water down the juice to decrease the sweetness. However, like fruit juices, most fruit and vegetable purees are also over-sweetened versions of the real food. With the exception of a few purees such as green beans, most taste much sweeter than the whole versions.

A 2012 study published in the *British Medical Journal* found that babies who were spoon-fed exclusively for the first four to six months of life had a higher preference for sweeter foods. There are benefits to purees, but their importance should be minimized in order to increase your child's palate for a variety of healthy foods. Children who are self-fed, and are offered whole foods early, have a significantly increased liking for whole grains, veggies, and healthier carbohydrates.

SELF-FEEDING CAN REDUCE OBESITY RISKS

In addition to promoting a wide variety of tastes in your child's diet, baby self-feeding promotes healthier physical eating habits by helping babies listen to their internal hunger cues. This way they can learn to eat when they are hungry and stop eating when they become full.

"Self-feeding naturally encourages responsive feeding, which promotes healthier eating patterns," says Brown. In her research, she found that children who were weaned using a baby-led approach were significantly more responsive to satiety and better able to regulate their own food intake later in life.

Allowing infants to choose which food they want to grasp and bring to their mouth is optimal for the development of satiety responsiveness. No longer is the parent deciding the pace and duration of each meal, which helps you teach your child how to determine the end point of a meal. When parents spoon-feed a child purees, they are consciously or subconsciously setting the portion sizes for him. The child doesn't learn how to control the pace of a meal and the amount of food his body needs. We have become used to food being widely available (often to the degree of being excessive). Feeling satiety and knowing when to stop eating are important skills to develop at a young age.

Baby self-feeding is a viable approach for early obesity prevention. In Brown's research, she found that children who were introduced to solids via baby-led weaning were less likely to be overweight compared with those who were fed exclusively purees with a spoon. They also had better appetite control.

When the infants started Brown's study at 6 to 12 months of age, they were all within a similar, average weight range. After one year, the toddlers in the spoon-fed group were significantly heavier than those in the self-feeding group. They were also more likely to be overweight. One year after the introduction of food, children who were only spoon-fed purees weighed an average of 2.4 pounds more than those who were introduced solids through baby-led weaning. While 8.1 percent of the baby-led weaning group weighed more than was recommended for their age, a staggering 19.2 percent of the spoon-fed children were deemed overweight. This relationship was independent of birth weight, breastfeeding duration, and age of introduction to solid foods. Other studies found similar results.

> A BABY WHO SELF-SELECTS, GRASPS, AND BRINGS FOOD TO HER MOUTH LEARNS HOW TO SELF-REGULATE HER FOOD INTAKE FROM A YOUNG AGE AND HAS A REDUCED RISK OF OBESITY LATER IN LIFE.

BUILDING YOUR BABY'S RELATIONSHIP WITH FOOD

In terms of lasting health implications, there are two primary benefits to the baby self-feeding approach: being able to introduce a variety of whole foods to the baby's diet and reducing the amount of parental control required. "It's always nicer to feed yourself than be spoon-fed," says Brown. "Babies are likely happier when they get to feel and play with the food and try things in their own time." Involving the baby creates a more positive relationship with food.

While early purees play a role in teaching your baby to swallow, when a caregiver exclusively spoon-feeds purees to a baby beyond a month or two, the baby does not have the same ability to explore and enjoy the food. By putting the baby in charge of the feeding process, it teaches him to use his instincts. The baby decides which food item to select, how much of it to consume, and the pace of the meal. The child also learns developmental skills on pinching and grasping foods and fitting in with family at the dinner table.

A FLEXIBLE APPROACH TO FIRST FOODS

Baby self-feeding is a revolutionary new approach to feeding your baby. It reflects a long evolution of baby feeding and proven methods for teaching children to eat. It is a more flexible program using the best lessons and practices from other programs, methods, and traditions. Baby self-feeding offers a realistic approach to feeding. The flexibility of the program gives parents permission to skip a section if it's not working for their child, while the variety gives your child the tools to love food and enjoy exploring new tastes and textures. It's a healthy way to get maximum nutrients, while teaching proper swallowing techniques that will minimize gagging and reduce the fear of choking.

A Successful Feeding Solution

- Baby-led weaning teaches children to go straight to solid foods, skipping the puree stage. However, research shows there are benefits to flexibility in early feeding practices, rather than sticking to one strict regimen.

- Baby-self feeding is a flexible feeding model that encourages limited purees mixed with finger foods. Babies get all the proven benefits of baby-led weaning without the increased gagging and fears of choking.

- Offering a variety of foods from day one helps create an adventurous eater.

- The key to reducing picky eating is variety and involving your baby in the feeding process from day one.

- The more tastes and textures you can expose your child to from an early age, the better.

- Feeding your child exclusive purees for too long can create a preference for sweeter foods, and may even contribute to obesity down the road.

- Your child should be an active participant in the feeding process from day one in order to help build a healthy relationship with food.

- CHAPTER 2 -

Early Nutritional Guidance: Encouraging Adventurous and Healthy Eaters

You don't need to look further than your local school to see that there is something wrong with the way kids eat today. When it comes to food, the expectations we set for our kids are very different from those many adults set for themselves.

Although we may start with good intentions of feeding baby pureed fruits and vegetables, for many children their diet soon evolves into a smorgasbord of "kid food," such as salty white crackers, gummies disguised as fruit, and French fries. For many parents, it comes to the point where we are happy if our child will actually eat a breaded chicken finger because at least she's getting a little protein.

The Disappearing Cracker

Fish-shaped crackers that crunch and melt in baby's mouth are fine as an early practice food, but don't let your child depend on these. Marjorie Meyer Palmer, M.A., CCC-SLP, reports that children who are able to chew may still "avoid fresh fruits, vegetables, and meats that do not dissolve in the mouth and prefer to eat crispy, crunchy food that melt easily.

Your goal should be to offer your child the flavors and tastes you'd like him to eat when he's older as soon as he starts to eat. As a parent, you won't always be able to control the food that is presented to your child. He'll be offered doughnuts and juice boxes after a sports practice and cupcakes at every birthday party and special event. Your job is to encourage your child from an early age to crave healthy foods and to appreciate variety in his diet. We're not saying he'll never join in the chocolate cake at a party. However, if your child grows up always being given a variety of foods, his taste palate will be trained not to favor traditional "kid's fare" for the mainstay of his diet.

A Love Affair with Sugar

Today, adults seem to reward all kinds of events, large and small, with sugar. When we grew up, we had the occasional birthday party with cake, Halloween treats, or summer ice cream cones. These days sugar is practically its own food group. Processed foods are dished out in kids' lunchboxes (because it's "the only thing my kid will eat") and at play dates. Birthday parties, which seem to happen every week, have not only cake, but also loot bags filled with candy and often other party treats. Then there's school. Many kids bring birthday treats to school on the actual day of their celebration, and there are class parties, fairs, and cookie day fundraisers. Nancy's son is even in a reading club where a well-meaning teacher rewards the kids with mini chocolate bars for a job well done. Kids are conditioned to expect sugary treats as a reward, only strengthening their love affair with sugar.

The outcome is our kids eat too much sugar. Results from the National Health and Nutrition Examination Survey (NCHS) found that American boys ages 12 to 19 years of age consume an average of 442 sugar calories a day. Although this was the age group with the highest sugar consumption, all of the age groups tested ate more sugar than is healthy. The average added sugar intake among all age groups in the study (ages 2 through 19) was 16 percent of a child's total caloric intake. Our kids are wasting too many of their calories on sugar and are paying the price with decreased attention spans, skyrocketing obesity rates, and negative health implications.

While we all have a soft spot for sweets, children tend to prefer higher concentrations of sugar than adults do. It's been argued that our children are wired to prefer sweets, that it's part of a survival instinct. After all, breast milk is sweet. But although an increased desire for sweets may have been beneficial before the days of processed sugar, it is now counterproductive. Because manufactured sugary foods trump natural food in sweetness, kids tend to gravitate to packaged foods and candy.

Since children have a natural propensity to be drawn to foods with added sugars, it's our job as parents to help steer their taste buds toward other healthier flavors from an early age. Although we can't completely override a desire for sweets, we can introduce many different healthy tastes and textures as early as possible.

As your child gets older it will become increasingly difficult to monitor the foods that are offered to him. Although sugary treats were at one time offered sporadically, they have now become commonplace in our culture and our diets. But as a parent, you can make a difference in how much sugar your child's body is exposed to from the very start.

SUGAR IS EVERYWHERE

Every time you pay for gas, buy a magazine, or wait in line at the grocery store, you find yourself surrounded by candy, other sweets, and sugary drinks. It is not uncommon for grocery and big box stores to feature a cooler at the beginning of every checkout lane filled with bottles of soda. An impulse buy of just one can of pop adds 40 grams of sugar (or 8 teaspoons) to an adult's diet. That's 2 teaspoons (10 g) more than what the American Heart Association recommends for an adult woman in a full day. Just think of what that amount means for a child.

It can be difficult as a parent not to give in when a toddler whines or screams for a treat in the checkout line. However, the American Heart Association (AHA) recommends that toddlers consume no more than 17 grams (about 4 teaspoons) of added sugar per day. That's the amount in just roughly half a candy bar. Our society has placed parents in a position of constantly having to say no or paying the price with health complications down the road.

RESIST YOUR CHILD'S SWEET TOOTH

You'll find that given the choice, most children prefer sweet foods. "This desire is likely directly related to growth patterns," says Alison Ventura, an assistant professor at California Polytechnic State University. Sweet foods are associated with calories, and it's natural to have a strong desire for sweetness during large growth spurts. Before the age of processed foods and the abundance of sugar, this preference was less problematic. However, a desire for a piece of fruit is different than the desire for a cookie.

"Don't cater to your child's desire for sweetness just because that's what he seems to prefer," says Ventura. If you give in to your baby's desire for sweet foods, you're only reinforcing negative

Limit Processed and Natural Sugars

Limit your child's exposure to all added sugars from the time you first introduce foods. This includes sugar naturally present in honey, syrups, fruit juices, and fruit concentrates.

nutritional programing. Added sugar is not beneficial or necessary for your children's growth or development. That's not to say your child can't have some sweet foods, but you should continue to offer variety during this time period and encourage healthier options.

Kids Love Salt, Too

Just as people have cravings for sweets, most of them also have cravings for salty foods. This is no different for kids. This is the driving force between the popularity of fish-shaped crackers and other similar snacks. The driving taste is salt.

Experts feel that a young child's desire for salty tastes, much like a child's desire for sugar, comes from ingrained survival instincts. Sodium used to be rare, and kids were drawn to salty tastes in order to get the minerals needed for bone growth. Since salt is now so plentiful in restaurants and packaged foods, it's important that parents do what they can to limit salt in their child's diet. The average daily sodium intake for 4- to 13-year-old children is approximately 3,200 milligrams (excluding table salt). This is well above the adequate (and recommended) level of 1,200 to 1,500 milligrams per day.

Recommended Sugar Intake

The World Health Organization recommends keeping daily sugar intake below 10 percent of our total daily caloric intake, with 5 percent being the ideal target for good health. Depending on activity levels, a toddler needs about 1,200 calories a day. That means just 60 to 120 calories should come from sugar. One tablespoon of maple syrup and a chocolate-covered granola bar each have about 100 sugar calories.

Boost Veggie and Fruit Intake

According to 2015 research published in *Appetite*, just 20 percent of children get the recommended 5 daily servings of fruit and vegetables. Most school-aged children eat just one portion of vegetables each day, and 7 percent of children eat no fruit or vegetables.

Interventions later in childhood are difficult. If kids don't like produce by the time they start school, it can be challenging to make significant changes. Interventions at school aimed at promoting fruit and vegetable intake have a relatively low success rate, with an average of only 0.07 grams of additional vegetables eaten each day. We applaud such efforts, but also stress the importance of starting young.

Food preferences developed at an early age can influence nutritional patterns for years to come. If you want kids and teens to eat fruits and vegetables, introduce these foods on a regular basis early in life. The first two years of life are especially crucial in terms of developing healthy eating habits. There is a window of opportunity during this time period in which new foods are more easily accepted. Once food habits are established, they have a tendency to stabilize—whether they're healthful or not.

If you want your child to eat well and have a diet rich in fruits and vegetables, it's also imperative that you do the same. Studies have found that kids tend to follow their parents' lead when it comes to healthy eating, especially in early years. Parents have a tremendous influence over how many fruits and vegetables their children will eat, so set the proper example.

The Making of a Favorite Food

One serving of fish-shaped crackers contains 10 percent of the recommended daily amount (RDA) of salt for adults! Plus, crackers are simple carbohydrates and are easily converted into sugar in the digestive tract. That conversion to oh-so-satisfying sugar seals the deal. Most crackers are "meltable," meaning they combine with the saliva in our mouths and just melt away, requiring very little chewing. Thus, they are a favorite first food to give to babies. Early and consistent exposure, combined with the preferred tastes of salt and sugar, make these a favored food for kids if they are given the choice.

Family Mealtimes with Hectic Schedules

Another problematic issue regarding child nutrition is not just what they eat but also how they eat. Families are often eating on the run and have less time to share a meal together. When they do eat together, they may be disconnected or distracted by electronics. Though it can be difficult to carve out family mealtime, it is crucial for your child's nutritional development—even if you cannot make it happen every day.

Take time for a family meal from the moment you start feeding your baby solid foods. Kids who share in a family meal tend to eat healthier and eat more fruits and vegetables. Understandably, people are busy and may not be able to eat as a family every night. However, even sharing in a family meal once or twice a week is enough to significantly increase a love of vegetables. That's a terrific start!

A study from the University of Leeds found that children who always engaged in a family meal together at the table ate an average of 1.5 portions (125 grams) more fruits and vegetables than children who never ate with their families. However, even families who ate together only once or twice a week had kids who consumed 1.2 portions (95 grams) more fruits and veggies. Just the act of sharing a family meal and eating healthy foods will improve the quality of your children's diet.

ENGAGING YOUR CHILD IN MEALTIME

"All activity builds the brain connection," says Eileen Viloria-Tan, a parenting supervisor at Peel Public Health. Any movement is a critical factor in the development of gross and fine motor skills, as well as cognitive skills such as language and the ability to pay attention. Parents should aim to make their children an active part of their daily activities—especially mealtime.

"Being an active part of the family mealtime builds brain skills and develops fine motor skills," says Doreen Bolhuis, president of Gymco, Inc., and an appointed member of the Governor's Council for Physical Fitness, Health and Sport for Michigan. "Babies are capable of more than being a passive participant."

Make Healthy Choices Early for Long-Term Results

Starting to feed your baby solid foods is an exciting time! Keep it stimulating by encouraging him to try a variety of healthy tastes and textures and feed himself. When you're choosing the foods your baby will eat, look ahead and focus on how you want him to eat as an older child and even as a teen and an adult. "When you choose how and what you'll feed your baby, you are laying down pathways for what your baby will prefer later in life," says Bolhuis.

Think of learning to eat like learning a new language. If you speak only English to your child for the first two years of her life, then that will become her preferred language and the one that will be easiest for her to learn. Later on, let's say your child wants to learn Spanish. She will be able to do it, but it will not come as naturally as English without much more work. Without true dedication, your child will may revert back to English and lose her path to learning a new language.

> FOOD PREFERENCES DEVELOPED AT AN EARLY AGE CAN INFLUENCE NUTRITIONAL PATTERNS FOR YEARS TO COME.

Eating preferences are similar to language. Just like your mind is programmed early for language and speech perception, your brain is programmed with taste preferences. It's up to parents to ensure that vegetables, textures, and even spices are part of the preferred "food language" for their child. "Don't make the healthy options a major effort for your child," says Bolhuis. Program the pathways in the brain to prefer a variety of healthy foods, and downplay the natural predisposition toward sweetness and salt.

EARLY NUTRITION MATTERS

Why do some children gleefully gobble up broccoli while others insist on a diet that consists almost solely of bread with butter and cereal? It seems equally unfair that some people seem to be able to eat whatever they want without gaining an unwanted pound, while others tend to turn every extra sugary morsel of food into unwanted body fat.

On the one hand, metabolism and taste preferences are both determined in part by genetics. People are born with different body shapes, and some people are just naturally thinner than others. A study out of Laval University found that genetics plays a significant role in both our propensity to hold on to body fat and where that body fat is located. In fact, genetics can increase your chances of holding on to fat in the abdominal region by about 50 percent.

There are also genetic variations in the foods we desire. While most people are naturally drawn to sweet foods, people who have an inherent bitter taste sensitivity are more reluctant to accept the taste of bitter foods, including many vegetables. Some kids have a greater genetic sensitivity to bitterness and, as a result, a decreased preference for bitter vegetables, grapefruit, and soy products. This can be overcome; however, it is even more crucial to introduce proper feeding practices with these kids at an early age. If children with bitter taste sensitivities are fed purees and bland foods for too long, they can have difficulty adjusting to other flavors and textures later on.

How our children experience foods in the early years may be even more crucial than genetics in terms of shaping their desired food tastes, metabolism, and propensity to hold on to body fat. Research shows that our early diets can have an impact on the way our body holds on to fat later in life. Likewise, innate taste preferences can be overridden, particularly if the tastes in question are introduced early in a child's eating experience. It seems early diets may do a lot more than fill up bellies and provide nutrients. Our children's first experiences with food can have lasting implications on their taste preferences and their ability to maintain a healthy weight later in life.

Common Problems in Kids' Diets

- The average child gets 16 percent of her daily caloric intake from sugar.
- Parents use high-sugar, processed foods to reward children.
- Children have a tendency to prefer higher concentrations of sugar and salt than adults do.
- Just 20 percent of children get the recommended 5 daily servings of fruits and vegetables.
- Many children are disengaged from the food they eat and are often disconnected from their family and friends during mealtime.

SENSITIVE PERIODS OF FOOD LEARNING

Researchers believe there may be critical windows in early development during which nutrition choices, and the way in which food is presented, could have long-term consequences on both the way our bodies respond to food and the way we eat for the rest of our lives. For example, it has been proven that there are visual and auditory windows of opportunity, or sensitive time periods, when neural sensitivity is higher, and researchers believe that there is also a window of opportunity for taste preferences.

Early exposure to certain flavors or foods and the way in which foods are presented can change the way the body reacts to food and help override certain genetic taste preferences. It can even impact the way our body processes and holds on to the foods we eat. In essence, our first tastes can play a strong role in the food and flavor choices we desire in the future and how we process the food we eat.

Encourage Healthy Eating from a Young Age

- Introduce a variety of healthy tastes and textures from the moment you start feeding your child solid foods.
- Instill healthy eating habits during the first two years of life, a crucial period in child development.
- Children tend to model their parents' eating behaviors, so parents should eat plenty of fruits and veggies, too.
- Sharing in a family meal once or twice a week is enough to significantly increase produce intake.

- Parents should aim to make their children an active part of mealtime from the moment they start eating solid foods.
- Being an active part of family mealtime builds brain skills and helps develop fine motor skills.
- When choosing the foods your baby will eat, focus on how you want her to eat as an older child and even as a teen.

NUTRITIONAL PROGRAMMING

The types of foods we choose to feed our child are a form of nutritional programming. This programming helps set the stage for dietary preferences and metabolic effects in the future.

Nutritional programming has been convincingly demonstrated in animals in numerous studies. The first research dates back to the 1960s, when Robert McCance, a founding member of the Nutrition Society and a professor at Cambridge University, showed that early nutrition could have a lifetime of programming effects. In his studies, McCance manipulated the litter size in rats so that rats from large litters received less breast milk than those from small litters during a 21-day suckling period. At the end of the first 21 days of life, the rats from the large litters that were fed less were substantially smaller than those from smaller litters that received more breast milk. No huge surprise here; eating more results in gaining more weight. But here's where things start to get interesting.

After the initial 21-day period, both groups were fed similar, normal intakes of food. However, the smaller animals (who initially came from the large litters) continued to be smaller than the animals that were initially fed more milk. This initial three-week dietary intervention resulted in a lifetime of programmed growth trajectory. How much the rats were fed during the initial three-week period of neural sensitivity impacted their body size for the rest of their lives.

SOME KIDS HAVE A GREATER GENETIC SENSITIVITY TO BITTERNESS AND, AS A RESULT, A DECREASED PREFERENCE FOR BITTER VEGETABLES, GRAPEFRUIT, AND SOY PRODUCTS.

Researchers then set about adapting the diet of groups of rats at different stages of their lives. However, when dietary manipulation happened after the initial three weeks of life, it had no lasting effect. If animals were underfed food for any period after the first 21 days of life, they quickly caught up with the growth patterns of the other animals after they were re-fed at a similar rate. Only the diet in the first three weeks of life, or the period of neural sensitivity, had a lasting nutritional programming impact.

A number of animal studies have followed these early findings by McCance, and scientists have demonstrated a wide variety of nutritional programming effects on not just future growth and obesity risks but also on metabolism, taste preferences, blood pressure, diabetes, atherosclerosis, behavior, and even learning. One interesting study in early programming and its effects on obesity later in life was done on baboons in the 1980s. Researchers from the University of Texas Health Center found that overfeeding in infancy resulted in obesity later in life. In the study, newborn baboons were fed Similac formulas with varying caloric densities for the first 16 weeks of life. One group was fed less than the daily recommended calories, one group was fed the daily recommended calories, and the last group was fed more than the daily recommended calories. Then, from 16 weeks until 5 years of life all of the baboons were fed the same diet. Although the overfed baboons were temporarily overweight during the overfeeding period, they returned to a normal weight throughout their

Neural Sensitivity and New Habits

Certain developmental time periods are considered to be "neurally sensitive" in that the brain is more highly wired to accept and process new information and experiences. Exposures during this heightened period of neural sensitivity will impact the function of the brain and body in the future. Exposure to stimuli during a sensitive neural period will have a stronger and more pronounced imprinting effect than these same experiences would have during another stage of life, and they have the capacity to induce lasting changes in an individual's behavior and underlying sensory and neural function. One of the periods of neural sensitivity is in the first year of life. Tastes introduced before the age of one will be easier to accept than those introduced later. The window will open again, but parents will need to do a bit of guesswork when offering healthy foods at regular time intervals until they finally become accepted.

childhood. However, the baboons that were overfed as infants became overweight in adolescence and the effects lasted into adulthood. The hypothesis is that early nutrition influences the number of adult fat cells and that overfeeding during a critical period of neural sensitivity will have a lasting impact on weight in the future.

In another study, baboons were randomly assigned to breastfeeding or formula, and then both groups were placed on a Western-style high-saturated-fat diet. In adulthood, the group of baboons who had breastfed during the period of neural sensitivity had healthier cholesterol levels than the formula-fed group.

For obvious reasons, nutritional programming hasn't been as easy to prove in humans. It's difficult to find an ethical way to adapt human diets and even more difficult to track with accuracy. However, the theory is that, similar to animals, humans have a sensitive time period during which nutritional programming can occur. And although exact periods of neural sensitivity are unclear, most experts agree that the time your baby first gets his first taste of solid food—around six months—is a critical window for developing taste preferences. "Up to six months of age is a really crucial period in terms of nutritional programming," says Ventura.

Also, certain foods eaten by a mother during pregnancy and breastfeeding can impact a child's taste preferences. "However, any favorable taste preferences that your child may get from a mother who ate lots of fruits and vegetables and flavorful foods during pregnancy and breastfeeding will be lost if these same foods are not introduced to the child." So while it's important to feed your child a healthy, nutrition-packed diet at all times, providing a healthy diet, in the right proportions, in the first year may be especially significant.

TASTE PREFERENCES BEGIN BEFORE BIRTH

Nancy's husband has always said that their children's insatiable desire for chocolate comes from her almost daily chocolate intake during her three pregnancies. "It's like the kids were programed to crave chocolate," he says. Well, maybe they were.

Researchers have found that the ability to perceive flavors begins before birth with the development and early functioning of the gustatory and olfactory systems in utero. Amniotic fluid surrounds the fetus and is a rich source of sensory exposure for the growing infant. Since a mother's amniotic fluid contains molecules derived from her diet, what a mother eats during her pregnancy can have an impact on her child's perception of taste and smell.

In particular, some studies have detected odors and compounds of garlic, cumin, and curry in the amniotic fluid. Since a child regularly swallows and smells amniotic fluid, these are in essence the first food experiences your baby will have. It has also been proven that women who eat a lot of certain strong tastes, such as curry and garlic, during their pregnancies have babies who readily accept this as a first taste when they are given solid food. A child's development of taste continues after birth with breastfeeding or formula. Like amniotic fluid, breast milk contains molecules derived from a mother's diet.

Dr. Julie Mennella is a member of Monell Chemical Senses Center and one of the leading experts in studying the role of early taste experiences and their impact on food and flavor preferences and growth later in life. In one of her more famous studies, Mennella set out to determine whether introducing certain foods into a mother's diet could establish a dietary preference in her baby. She asked pregnant moms to drink either 300 milliliters of carrot juice or water for four days a week for three consecutive weeks during the third trimester. The women were asked to do the same during the first two months of breastfeeding. Just prior to six months of age, the babies in the study were given both cereal prepared with water and cereal prepared with carrot juice. None of the infants had ever been fed carrot juice or any foods containing carrots before. The babies' reactions were videotaped. The babies who had been exposed to carrots during pregnancy and breastfeeding were perceived to enjoy the carrot-flavored cereal more, had happier expressions, and were more willing to eat the carrot-flavored cereal.

"Early flavor experiences appear to shape early food preferences," says Ventura, who has also done extensive research on the subject. The influence of these preferences appears to extend into early childhood and translates to later food preferences, making prenatal and early postnatal periods neurally sensitive periods for early flavor and food preference learning.

DON'T BE AFRAID OF NEW AND VIBRANT FLAVORS

While we can control the tastes and nutrients a baby gets while in utero and via breast milk, controlling what they will actually eat when we introduce solid foods is somewhat more difficult. When solid foods are introduced around six months, you need to offer your child a variety of healthy tastes and textures to help maintain any positive effect the foods you've eaten during pregnancy and nursing have had on your child's developing taste preferences. Plus, these first solid food choices will have a large impact in their own right.

It's important not to fall into the pattern of feeding your baby bland, mostly pureed foods from 6 to 12 months of age. "Many parents are surprised by the notion that you could give an 8-month-old Thai food," says Ventura. Although foods need to be an appropriate size and texture for a baby in terms of safety, your child can handle spices and a large variety of foods from a young age. Babies who live off purees in a pouch, Cheerios, and toast turn into toddlers and children with these same taste preferences. Feed your baby the safe foods that you want your child to eat, not the foods that you've been led to believe are appropriate for a baby.

Avoid Overfeeding Your Baby

Obesity's causes and risks have been well documented in animals, and it's hypothesized that the impact is similar in humans. Certain nutrients may provide critical signals that program key metabolic pathways. Feeding your child the right amount of healthy foods at an early age may have a positive impact on long-term metabolism. Likewise, it's believed that overfeeding in the early years may have a lasting impact on the development of fat cells. Eating too much during a period of neural sensitivity can increase the number of fat cells in the body and those fat cells won't decrease, even if the feeding pattern returns to normal.

Breastfeeding is ideal because it lets your child self-regulate her food intake. With formula it's easier to overfeed your baby. She will learn to finish a bottle even when she may not be hungry. Just like you, babies will be hungrier at certain meals than at others. During periods of more growth or neural development, your child will need more food. If you are formula feeding, listen to your baby's cues, such as disinterest, turning her head away, and distracted behavior. Resist the urge to always finish the bottle. If you can put it away without your baby fussing to get it back, she is likely full. As long as your baby is happy and continuing to grow at the projected rate, chances are she's getting enough food.

Once your baby turns to solid food, you also need to listen to her cues as to when to eat and when not to eat. Overfeeding now can lead to obesity in your child's teens or in adulthood. After all, it's estimated that 23 percent of infants ages 7 to 11 months eat more than the required amount of food. This is often the case when parents fail to carefully regulate the amount of food babies eat.

Continue to Offer Foods That Kids Dislike

If you offer your child a healthy food and he doesn't like it, don't give up. Studies show that repeated exposure to a disliked food will help promote the acceptance of, and eventual preference for, that food. Sometimes kids turn up their noses at new foods and parents might give up too quickly. In fact, a national study of more than 3,000 infants found that most parents drew conclusions as to whether or not their child liked a certain food after just one or two feeding attempts. Parents are often too quick to determine that their child doesn't like a particular food, flavor, or texture.

Repeated exposure can help get your child to like a particular food, but it takes time. Studies show that a child may need to be exposed to a new food 8 to 15 times before accepting it. The key word is "accepting." Liking and loving some foods may require even more taste testing over time.

The research is out as to whether repeated mere exposure to a new food is enough to win a reluctant child over. While some experts insist that exposure must include tasting the food, as opposed to merely seeing or learning about a new food, others disagree. A recent study found that repeatedly exposing children to a novel food within a positive social environment was highly effective in increasing their willingness to try the new food, and it helped increase their liking for the new food.

A landmark University of Michigan study found that there is a direct correlation between the availability and exposure of vegetables and children's average preference ratings. The study took place in the late 1960s and found that the top seven most available and talked about foods at the time—corn, potatoes, lettuce, carrots, asparagus, cauliflower, and broccoli—were also rated as the most preferred (in the same order). It seems that at any age mere repeated exposure to something enhances our attitude toward it.

Parents should lead by example and eat the foods they would like their children to eat. They can engage their children in shopping and food preparation, too. Continue to place a small amount of the shunned healthy food on your child's plate. Don't make it a fight, and if they don't eat it, it's okay. The first step may be leaving the food on the plate, the next step may be one bite. Over time, children can work their way up to accepting foods they once hated. Research shows that the more times you try something, the more you will generally like it. This mere exposure effect has been shown in everything from food and art to unfamiliar music and languages.

DON'T PRESSURE FEED

For repeated exposure to be effective, you must resist pressure tactics and offer food in a positive, nonjudgmental environment. If children are pressured to try certain foods on a regular basis, the effect can be the opposite of what is desired. Not only will your child be unlikely to take to foods when pressured, but he may also harbor lasting negative feelings toward the food and show a decreased preference for that food.

Melanie is witness to the stress that parents face when their child has trouble eating. With the best of intent, these parents feel the need to get calories into their baby in order for her to grow. Unfortunately, the extreme stress can cloud a parent's thinking and it's often challenging for them to see the bigger picture. If your anxiety around your child's eating habits, even in the first year of life, causes you to urge her to take another bite, another bite, and yet another bite, then please seek support from a qualified feeding therapist. A speech-language pathologist (SLP) or an occupational therapist (OT) can determine why your child is having difficulty, thus taking the pressure off you to get calories in and taking the pressure off your child to eat. Once the "why" is addressed, parents slowly relax and the kids do, too. Tasting new foods becomes easier and repeated exposures work. However, repeated exposure shouldn't be pushy. Simply present the food and gently encourage your child to interact with it. It's best not to say "take a bite" but instead to chat about the characteristics of the food, such as the crunch or aroma. With enough exposures, your child will taste it in her own time when she is ready.

EXPOSE BABIES TO NEW FOODS EARLY AND REPEATEDLY

Because there is an early period of neural sensitivity when it is easier to urge the acceptance of new foods, it makes sense that there is also a window of opportunity when repeated exposure to foods is likely to be more effective in winning kids over. That being said, there is evidence of sensitive periods appearing later in life, where repeated exposure to certain foods can be highly effective. So if you have an older child who shuns broccoli, don't give up. While he may not be receptive to repeated exposure tactics at age four, a window of neural sensitivity may open again at five.

Besides, repeated exposure can be highly effective at any age under the right circumstances. Think of your first experience with coffee, for example. If you're like most people, you didn't enjoy it the first time you tried it. But at some point, you drank it again. Chances are you may not have liked it the second or third time, either. But for some reason you kept drinking coffee. We are quite certain your parents didn't force you to drink coffee; you decided to keep trying it on your own. Likely it had something to do with mere exposure to people drinking coffee and their positive associations with coffee or hearing about positive effects of caffeine. Whatever the reason, you kept drinking coffee, and like many of us, grew to not only like it but also to make it an essential part of your life. Coffee is an extremely bitter beverage. It doesn't get any less bitter with time, but through repeated exposure the brain learns that coffee is not harmful and that your body even likes the effects of it. Through repeated exposure you learned to like, possibly even rely on, a bitter drink that you originally did not like. As a society we have come to love this bitter beverage, and it is proof that repeated exposure can be highly beneficial.

The Importance of Making Healthy Feeding Choices Early

- While genetics plays a role in both weight and food preferences, your child's early food experiences can be even more crucial in terms of shaping his future food preferences and even his metabolism and risk of obesity.

- Taste preferences start to develop before birth.

- Children have a heightened neural sensitivity in the first year of life. During this time it is crucial to introduce a variety of healthy foods to your child, in the right quantities.

- Don't cater to your child's desire for sweetness just because that's what she seems to prefer.

- Listen to your baby's cues on when he's hungry and avoid overfeeding.

- Repeated exposure can help get your child to like a particular food, but it takes time. Your child may need to be exposed to a new food 8 to 15 times before accepting it.

- Feed your baby the safe foods that you want your child to eat in the future, not the foods that you've been led to believe are appropriate for a baby.

CHAPTER 3

Weaning from the Breast or Bottle

For most babies, six months is the ideal time to start introducing solid foods. Since 2002, the World Health Organization (WHO) infant feeding guidelines recommend a duration of exclusive breastfeeding from birth to six months (an extension from previous guidelines ending at four to six months). Most other major organizations have made the same recommendations, and parents are now introducing solids later than they have in decades.

When babies start solid foods prior to six months of age most lack the gross motor, fine motor, and oral motor skills required to safely eat solid foods. At six months of age, however, infants are developmentally more advanced and most can handle purees as an introductory texture, while moving quickly to safe self-feeding and finger foods.

This chapter explains how to read your baby's reflex cues and determine when he's ready to start solid foods.

Reading Your Baby's Feeding Reflexes

From the moment you cuddle your baby in your arms for the very first time, oral reflexes communicate to your baby's brain how to find food and how to suck, swallow, and breathe in a coordinated fashion. In fact, seven different reflexes—rooting, suckling, tongue, swallowing, biting, transverse tongue, and gagging reflexes—will guide your child (along with your help) through the developmental process of learning to eat.

As your baby experiences these reflexive movements, he will learn how to make the same movements purposefully time and again, thereby controlling the movements with intention. Over time, the reflexes will appear to fade away or "integrate" into the nervous and motor systems. This doesn't mean they've disappeared, however. The brain has allowed "purposeful and learned" movements to take precedence.

Understanding these seven reflexes will help you make decisions on what and when to feed your baby.

ROOTING REFLEX

What: When something touches your baby's lips or cheeks, her mouth moves toward the stimulation.

When: Rooting is most active in the first month of life.

Why: Helps locate the breast or bottle nipple for food and helps the hands and fingers, because babies are not dexterous yet, for early mouthing experiences.

Foods that are ideal for learning from this reflex: Liquids—breast milk or formula.

When you'll gradually see this same movement, but intentionally: After one month of age, your baby will turn toward the breast or the bottle and open his mouth to accept it willingly. The reflex fully integrates between three and six months of age.

SUCKLING REFLEX

What: A forward-backward wavelike tongue movement used to direct food down the throat. It's used to extract liquid from the breast or bottle and also for sucking on a pacifier, finger, or empty breast. Suckling morphs into sucking over time, which involves more advanced tongue movement, where the front of the tongue moves upward (i.e., independently from the rest of the tongue). The cheeks and lips engage even more and help propel a slightly heavier, larger, or thicker volume of food back to the throat to be swallowed.

When: Seen at birth; the baby gains control of suckle between two and three months.

Why: Suckling morphs into sucking so that babies can take in more volume from the breast or bottle with more coordination and less fatigue. This gain in coordination and strength is essential to learning to manage purees and soft solids.

Foods that are ideal for learning from this reflex: Liquids—breast milk or formula.

When you'll gradually see this same movement, but intentionally: Suckling continues to about two or three months of age and will gradually move to intentional sucking. Integrates between 6 and 12 months.

TONGUE REFLEX

What: A forward tongue motion that is likely part of the suckling reflex. It pushes food or objects out of the mouth.

When: Begins to fade around three or four months of age when baby develops sucking reflex.

Why: To protect airway as baby improves oral control over time.

Foods that are ideal for learning from this reflex: Liquids—breast milk or formula.

When you'll gradually see this same movement, but intentionally: The reflex starts to disappear around three or four months. Most pediatric feeding professionals report observing some intentional movement between six and nine months of age. This gray area makes it challenging to determine whether baby is intentionally pushing out the food or reflexively pushing out the food, and requires reading baby's communication cues to decide next steps in feeding. You will also observe the tongue reflex as your baby experiences new textures and shapes of food (or toys) between the ages of 12 and 18 months. By 18 months of age, the tongue reflex should be fully integrated and all forward movements of the tongue will be intentional. These gradual changes over time may come into play as you are introducing new foods, so continue to allow baby time to explore before assuming that he doesn't like a new food because he's "pushing it out of his mouth."

SWALLOWING REFLEX

What: A swallow occurs in three phases: oral (the food is prepped and chewed, then gathered to move back to the pharynx and throat region), pharyngeal (the food enters and travels down the throat), and esophageal (after the food goes down the throat and passes by the larynx or "voice box" and goes into the esophagus).

When: Begins in the womb.

Why: A swallow becomes more coordinated over time and morphs into a "mature swallow pattern" beginning around the age of 12 months. Babies begin to understand the concept of swallowing—and can do so purposely if you say "swallow"—beginning around 18 months of age.

Foods that are ideal for learning from this reflex: Liquids, purees of all textures, and baby early self-feeding foods (see chapter 5) should be introduced following the timeline of the other reflexes. The swallow continues to improve in coordination with exposure to different textures and types of foods, but only if introduced along the continuum of reflex integration and learning.

When you'll gradually see this same movement, but intentionally: Around 18 months of age.

BITING REFLEX

What: Baby will bite down and then release repeatedly on anything that applies gentle pressure to the gums.

When: Seen at birth, and begins to come under baby's control between 5 and 9 months when baby begins teething and receives safe foods of increasing texture; gradually integrates between 9 and 12 months of age.

Why: This jaw movement is separate from tongue movement, and eventually morphs into taking bites of and chewing food.

Foods that are ideal for learning from this reflex: Soft cookies or crackers that are meltable and early baby self-feeding foods.

When you'll gradually see this same motor movement, but intentionally: Between five and nine months baby begins to gain control and bite down on soft foods or chewy toys.

TRANSVERSE TONGUE REFLEX

What: Baby's tongue moves toward stimulation on the sides of the tongue.

When: Seen at birth and gradually integrates between 9 and 24 months of age.

Why: Needed for early steps to learn to control the food in her mouth; eventually, it's used to place food onto gums and later, on molars for chewing and to retrieve that same food in order to propel the food back and swallow.

Foods that are ideal for learning from this reflex: Long strips of handheld foods that stimulate the sides of the tongue as baby holds the rest of the strip in his fist. Chopped foods via spoon, finger, or dipper are perfect for this, too! The tongue needs to move laterally to build important muscles for feeding and speech.

When you'll gradually see this same movement, but intentionally: Control begins between six and eight months of age.

GAGGING REFLEX

What: The soft palate rises, the head may go back, the tongue lowers, and the jaw drops forward as the mouth opens wider. You may also see muscle contraction in the throat as the voice box rises.

When: The gag reflex remains throughout life, but moves farther back on the tongue so it is less likely to be stimulated. From six to nine months of age, the gag reflex is found on the back third of the tongue and eventually it will move to the back quarter of the tongue, depending on feeding experiences.

Why: It acts as a protective mechanism to prevent choking, although it's not foolproof.

Foods that are ideal for learning from this reflex: Purees and gradual introduction of baby self-feeding foods in order to ensure that negative feeding experiences are minimal.

When you'll gradually see this same movement, but intentionally: Never. Gags are always reflexive. However, they can become a conditioned response, where the brain associates the sight, sound, smell, or other sensory experiences with the thought of a certain food or object.

Don't Rush Solid Foods

It's rare that a baby needs any solid food prior to the age of six months. "If you are exclusively breastfeeding up to six months it will give your baby extra protection against infection, along with providing all the nutrients your baby needs to thrive," says Dr. Jack Newman, a respected pediatrician and one of North America's foremost breastfeeding experts.

Regardless of whether your baby is being fed breast milk or infant formula, waiting until your baby is ready for food will save you a lot of time and effort.

Children need time to develop before gathering up the courage to interact with a new food. Although your intentions may be good, if you push food on your child before she is ready you may actually be conditioning your child not to eat.

Even if your child has mastered the necessary steps to start self-feeding, if she doesn't want to eat, don't push it. As long as your baby continues to drink breast milk or formula and continues to grow and develop you likely do not need to worry. In the first few months of learning to eat, most of a child's nutrition will continue to come from breast milk or formula anyway. But don't hesitate to have a clear discussion with your child's pediatrician if your baby has not demonstrated interest in solid foods, especially purees, by the end of seven months of age. The physician may refer you to a feeding specialist (typically an occupational therapist or speech-language pathologist who specializes in feeding disorders) to evaluate your child's readiness.

READING (AND MISREADING) HUNGER SIGNS

Parents often mistake some common baby behaviors as signs that their child is ready for solid foods. If your baby is chewing her fists, looking for extra milk feedings, or waking during the night, it does not necessarily mean that she is ready for solid foods. These are normal behaviors that may or may not be signs of hunger. Babies explore their mouths in a variety of ways and seek comfort at the breast even when they are not hungry. Waking in the night can occur for a variety of reasons, including discomfort, short sleep cycle, and of course, hunger.

If your baby is hungry, extra breast milk or formula feedings are usually enough to satisfy him until he has the coordination, strength, and developmental skills required to eat solid foods. It's best not to assume that your baby needs extra food prior to six months. If you are worried that your baby isn't getting enough food, visit your doctor or a lactation specialist and see whether there is a way you can satisfy your baby's needs through breast milk.

EXCEPTIONS FOR EAGER SELF-FEEDERS (YOUNGER THAN SIX MONTHS)

There are some cases when it may be beneficial to start food prior to six months. Trust your gut. If your baby is four or five months old, seems to be hungry, and can hold her head up, ask your doctor if you can offer purees. But, if your baby doesn't take them, she's not ready. If she does, continue with purees until your baby is about six months or until she has mastered the swallowing technique.

If your baby isn't continuing to gain weight at the expected rate, you should also speak with your doctor about starting on purees prior to six months of age. That being said, a different breastfeeding technique may also help.

"Aiming to increase your baby's breastfeeding intake should be your first step," says Dr. Newman. "It's the best step." If you feel you're not producing enough milk, however, Newman suggests supplementing with purees after four months rather than adding formula. "Besides, the breastfed baby digests solid foods better and earlier than the formula-fed baby because breast milk contains enzymes that help digest fats, proteins, and starch," adds Newman.

Weaning from Breast Milk

Most health societies, including the American Academy of Pediatrics, the Canadian Pediatric Society, and the World Health Organization (WHO), suggest exclusively breastfeeding until six months of age. Breast milk offers all of the nutrients your baby needs (with the exception of vitamin D) for the first half year of life. If you are unable to breastfeed, formula can take its place.

Around the half-year mark, breast milk alone will no longer satisfy all of your baby's nutritional needs. "A full-term baby will start requiring iron from other sources by six to nine months of age," says Dr. Newman.

If you wait too long to introduce solids, your baby may be reluctant to take them. "Babies who have not started solids by nine months may have a great difficulty accepting solid foods," says Newman. Six months is the ideal time to introduce solids as a complement to breast milk or formula. Your growing baby is ready for the added nutrition and eager to try new things. If you wait too long, your baby may be highly reluctant to try the new foods you offer.

Breast milk is widely acknowledged to be the most complete form of nutrition for infants, with benefits related to immunity, health, growth, and development. It's more economical than formula and is convenient because you always have your baby's food with you. Breastfeeding has a positive impact on intelligence tests, educational attainment, and later income. Breastfeeding can have an influence on your child's food choices, health, and weight gain later in life. Fortunately, there are also benefits for breastfed babies when it comes time to begin self-feeding.

BREASTFED BABIES ARE OFTEN MORE ADVENTUROUS EATERS

When parents choose formula, they typically stick with one brand over the course of feeding. That brand is formulated the same way, with the exact same nutrient composition and the same taste. Breast milk, however, presents new and different tastes to your baby at each feeding. Depending on the mother's diet, the nutrient and flavor content of breast milk changes continually. Nancy remembers her first son being a reluctant drinker after she ate broccoli, for example.

Food preferences are not solely determined by what the mother eats while she is nursing, however. Although it plays a role, there are still plenty of breastfeeding moms who nosh on daily salads only to find that their children shun greens of any variety. "Picky eating" is a term for kids who are resistant to trying new foods, but the types of picking eating, from merely hesitant to extremely selective, is a complicated matter and the causes are not always easy to tease out. However, just the act of breastfeeding does generally encourage more adventurous eaters. Since breastfed infants are exposed to a range of different of flavors, it prepares them for a variety of tastes when they eat solid foods. On the other hand, formula-fed babies become used to a consistent taste every day for nine months. As a result, breastfed babies are less likely to crave bland foods and more willing to try new and exciting tastes.

BREASTFED BABIES CAN OFTEN BETTER REGULATE THEIR FOOD INTAKE

Breastfeeding is the earliest form of self-feeding. Much like self-feeding with food, breastfeeding puts your baby in control of her food intake. When a baby breastfeeds, she is able to regulate when and how much milk she gets.

Your baby will have different food needs based on the amount of growth that is happening at a particular time, the climate conditions, how fussy she's been, new experiences that day, and how much sleep she has had. When you feed your baby from a bottle you are predetermining how much milk your child needs. She gets the same amount at every feeding, regardless of her needs at that particular time. Similar to a baby who is spoon-fed a specific amount of purees, a bottle-fed baby may be a more passive participant in the feeding process.

Breastfed infants regulate their nutrient intake from birth. Since there is lower maternal control during milk feeding, and the quantity of milk taken and the duration of feeding is led by the infant, breastfed infants learn early on how to self-regulate their nutrition intake. Breastfed babies get only the amount of milk their body is asking for at a particular feeding, rather than being delivered a specific amount of milk at regular intervals.

This early self-regulation has results that extend far beyond infancy. Studies have proven that breastfeeding promotes satiety responsiveness in childhood. A baby who learns to eat only when hungry and stop eating when full becomes a child who eats only when his body feels hunger and stops when that hunger has been satisfied. Because these children learn self-regulation of food at a young age, breastfed infants have a lower risk of childhood obesity, compared to infants who are bottle-fed with either formula or expressed milk.

Weaning from Formula

Both breastfeeding and self-feeding place the infant in control of her food intake. However, there's no reason that you can't have a successful self-feeder if you've been feeding your baby formula. Since you should offer your baby purees prior to the self-feeding process anyway, there's no reason to do anything different when offering first foods to a baby who has been fed formula from a bottle.

There are sensitive periods early in your baby's life when he is more willing and able to accept new flavors. Early exposure to a varied amount of healthy foods, tastes, and textures will reduce the risk of having a picky eater. If you have been feeding your child formula, it will be helpful to place him in the driver's seat and let him self-feed as soon as he is developmentally ready. Offer a variety of healthy foods and tastes, and don't get discouraged if your child doesn't take to them immediately. Be patient. Don't give up!

IF YOUR CHILD'S NOT PROGRESSING TO ANY PUREES AFTER SEVEN MONTHS OF AGE, SEEK THE HELP OF A FEEDING SPECIALIST.

However, if you feed your baby exclusive purees until nine months or later you may find that when you want to introduce varied tastes and textures you'll have problems with your child positively responding to them. Timing is key.

Formula-fed babies who move directly to a brief period of exclusive purees and then to early self-feeding tend to do very well in terms of self-regulation and eating varied foods later on in life. If, however, you follow up formula with an extended period of bland purees, in amounts that are predetermined by you, you may have issues both with food intake regulation and with a willingness to try new foods.

Continue Breastfeeding and/or Formula Until at Least Age One

You shouldn't feel the need to stop breastfeeding just because you introduce solids. In fact, your baby will continue to get most of her nutrition from breast milk or formula while she is learning how to manage table food.

Studies show continued benefits related to immunity, health, and brain development by breastfeeding up until a year. If possible, we encourage mothers to continue to breastfeed until their baby is at least a year of age. Many mothers continue for longer—it's an individual choice.

Reasons to stop may include inconvenience for women who have gone back to work, pain, or frequent night wakings. Your baby shouldn't be getting night feedings beyond six months.

If you choose to continue breastfeeding beyond 12 months, you also need to ensure that your baby is eating three solid meals a day and that he is not simply grazing on snacks and at the breast. Your baby needs to have proper mealtimes. Grazing on snacks and various breastfeedings through the day can impact growth because babies may not be getting adequate calories when they eat small amounts just to stave off a bit of hunger or to seek comfort at the breast. If, however, you have a schedule of breastfeeding in the morning, evening, and maybe once during the day—and it's working for mom and baby—then continue as long as it feels right for you, your baby, and your family.

There is no need to continue with formula past 12 months of age, unless recommended by your doctor. By this age, your child should be eating enough different foods to fulfill her nutritional requirements. You can switch to milk and water as primary beverages starting at one year of age.

BALANCING BREAST MILK OR FORMULA WITH SOLIDS

Realistically, your baby won't get a lot of solid food in the first few months of self-feeding. For the first two or three months, most of your baby's nutrition will continue to come from breast milk or formula.

When you're starting out with solids, schedule a couple of regular mealtimes. This will most likely be breakfast and dinner, but choose whatever times are easiest for your family to eat together. Additionally, continue with your baby's regular breastfeeding or formula schedule. It's best not to feed your baby breast milk or formula and solids at the same feeding. Your baby will be more comfortable with breast milk or formula and may revert to that if you offer it in addition to food. If your baby is thirsty at mealtime you can offer him a small amount of water with his meal. When your baby begins solid foods, it is then safe to offer water as well.

"Don't get too hung up on the balance between breast milk and solids," says Newman. "You'll find that it happens organically." Your child will likely continue with her regular breastfeeding schedule, and shorten feeding times as she learns to eat more solids. Or she may start to drop feedings.

Around eight or nine months your baby will start to reduce his breast milk or formula requirements, provided he is eating well. The amount will continue to decrease to a year of age. At that time, your child should be drinking about 24 ounces (710 ml) of breast milk or formula.

LISTEN TO YOUR BABY'S CUES

Avoid feeding your baby solids when she is overly hungry. Exploring the world of solid foods is a new and exciting experience. It can also be overwhelming to a baby who is tired, fussy, or starving for food. You'll experience the most success introducing solids when your child is alert and not overly hungry. If your baby is craving food she will want to go to the breast, which she associates with eating. If she eats a full meal at the breast or bottle prior to attempting to eat solids, she won't be hungry enough to explore the tastes of solid foods.

Ideally, you should breastfeed your baby 30 to 60 minutes prior to offering solid food. For example, you could breastfeed your baby upon waking and then eat breakfast together an hour later. Your baby will want food, without being overly hungry, and will have the patience to explore new tastes and textures.

If you are bottle-feeding your baby you could try giving your baby a small (third of normal size) bottle prior to starting solids. Afterward, you could give the baby another small bottle (a third to two-thirds of normal size depending on how much food he ate).

"Rather than watching the clock, it is recommended that a mother watch for signs that her newborn is hungry," says Newman. Use the same cues that you used when you were breastfeeding—the rooting reflex or chewing or sucking on hands or fingers. Crying is a very late cue that your baby is hungry, and many babies "go over the edge" and are hard to console once they are crying and hungry. At that point, solid foods are out of the question. It's about balance and timing and getting to know your baby's communication style.

Cup or Bottle?

When it comes time to wean your baby from the breast, many mothers attempt to transition their child to a bottle. While some babies will take to a bottle with ease, others can be highly resistant to an artificial nipple. It's better to avoid transitioning to a bottle after six months and go right to a cup. Since we suggest transitioning your baby off the bottle at around a year, you'll just be getting your child used to feeding with a bottle, only to take it away again in a few months.

If you allow your child to have a bottle past one year, and to become dependent on it for comfort, the bottle can become a habit that is difficult to break. This can impact your child's motor development because the sucking motion, where the baby's tongue is repeatedly kept from rising up to the alveolar ridge (the front of the roof of the mouth where we say "d"), is a motor pattern that should be gone by this point. Continued use of the bottle can delay a baby's oral motor skills that are necessary for continued advancement in learning to eat solid foods. An open cup or a straw cup is the ideal way to wean a breastfeeding baby. It can be offered to any baby over six months of age.

> COMFORT SUCKING ON SWEETENED DRINKS IS THE LEADING CAUSE OF TOOTH DECAY IN YOUNG CHILDREN.

SKIP THE SIPPY CUP

You can decide to move your baby to a lidded/sippy/trainer cup, a cup with a straw, or a traditional cup without a spout. There is no developmental need for a lidded cup with a leak-proof spout; it is simply less messy and may be easier for parents to deal with.

Sippy cups are convenient, but also confusing to kids who are trying to learn open cup and straw drinking. Because kids can tip a lidded cup up to the sky and drink, they tend to do the same with open cups and straw cups. So while you may save a little mess now, lidded cups can actually lead to confusion and the potential for spills in the future. Skip the lidded cup or limit its use. The transition will be that much smoother for everyone.

USE OPEN CUPS TO HELP BABIES LEARN TO SIP PROPERLY

Using a regular cup is a better complement to self-feeding because it enhances independence and teaches your baby feeding skills that he will use for the rest of his life. It also requires sipping behavior, rather than sucking that is similar to feeding from a bottle. Comfort sucking on sweetened drinks is the leading cause of tooth decay in young children. When you introduce a cup without a valve or spout you will help your baby learn to sip rather than suck, which is better for his teeth. Avoiding cups with hard extended spouts is also best. It's important that a child can lift up his tongue and develop the mature swallow pattern, and an extended, hard spout gets in the way, just like the nipple on a bottle.

To use a cup, start with a small amount of liquid in the cup and show your baby how to use it by bringing the cup to his lower lip and gently tipping the cup upward. Help your baby hold the cup at the beginning, and then encourage him to hold it on this own, with two hands at first. See page 199 for specifics on teaching open cup drinking.

If you decide that a traditional cup is too messy, a cup with a straw is an effective option. Your baby should be able to sit independently in order to use a straw— ideally around seven to nine months. A straw helps develop a mature swallow pattern and is less messy than an open cup. It's quick to master and is a fast way to get nutrients into your baby. Once your baby has learned to drink from a straw, cut the straw down so that the tip of the straw reaches the tip of baby's tongue. Too long of a straw acts like a sippy cup, preventing the tongue tip from rising up to the alveolar ridge. See page 176 for the specifics on teaching straw drinking.

Lidded Cup

If you opt for a lidded cup, you should avoid non-spill valves if possible, which encourage extended sipping and can lead to dental issues and even mouth development issues down the road. Sometimes these valves are recommended for a child with special needs or swallowing disorders, but otherwise we suggest skipping a valved cup.

The transition to a cup won't take much longer than to a bottle (in some cases, it's even shorter) and you don't have to worry about transitioning from a bottle to a cup in another few months.

Formula or Cow's Milk?

There has been a lot of publicity recently about not giving your baby cow's milk until at least nine months, and in many cases a year. "The breastfeeding baby can take some of his milk as cow's milk after about six months of age, especially if he is starting to take substantial amounts of a wide variety of solids as well," says Newman.

Cow's milk gets a bad rap because it does not offer sufficient nutrients as a primary food supply for your baby. However, if your baby is in the process of weaning and is still getting breast milk and is also eating solids, then there is no reason not to introduce cow's milk as a supplementary drink after six months. If your baby is no longer breastfeeding, however, you should feed her formula until a year. At that time, she will have mastered eating a varied diet and will not need the extra nutrients that breast milk and formula provide.

IF YOUR BABY IS STILL RECEIVING SOME BREAST MILK, AND IS EATING A WIDE VARIETY OF FOODS, YOU CAN ADD COW'S MILK OR GOAT'S MILK AS A SUPPLEMENTARY DRINK AFTER SIX MONTHS.

"Many breastfeeding babies will not drink formula because they do not like the taste," says Newman. If you are in the process of weaning, don't become overly concerned with adding formula. "The breastfeeding baby can get all the milk he needs from the breast, even if he is breastfeeding only a few times a day," continues Newman. As long as your baby is getting some breast milk and some food, you don't need to be overly concerned about adding formula.

Other Early Drinks

Once your baby is eating solids two or more times a day, he will start to take less milk at each feeding or drop milk feeding altogether. If possible, continue to offer the breast until your baby is at least one year of age. "Breastfeeding will continue to benefit you and your baby for as long as you carry on," says Newman.

Once breastfeeding starts to diminish you will need to supplement with other liquids. However, not all drinks are suitable for babies and young children. Here's a look at what you should, and shouldn't, give your baby to drink.

WATER

Water is a healthy way to quench your child's thirst. Fully breastfed babies don't need any water until they've started eating solid food. Bottle-fed babies may need some extra water in hot weather, but check with your pediatrician and ask about specific amounts for your baby depending on her nutritional needs, size, and the climate where you live.

Start good habits with water early. Always offer water as a beverage with meals if your child is thirsty and use it as the primary thirst quencher throughout the day.

DAIRY

Cow's milk is fine as an occasional supplement from 6 to 12 months of age, but it doesn't contain enough iron and other nutrients to meet young babies' needs as their primary drink. If you choose to give your baby cow's milk prior to a year, do so sparingly and continue to offer breast milk or formula as your baby's primary beverage.

You should opt for whole milk until your children is two years old, as a young child needs the extra energy and vitamins it contains. If you prefer, you can switch to 2 percent at two years of age, provided your child is a good eater and is growing well. Skim and 1 percent milk are not suitable for children under five, as they don't contain enough calories. Children should not be given unpasteurized milk because of the higher risk of food poisoning. If you prefer, you can offer goat or sheep's milk as an alternative; however, avoid rice drinks as they contain inorganic arsenic, which can be harmful in large doses.

FRUIT JUICES AND SMOOTHIES

Fruit juices are high in natural (and sometimes added) sugars and acids, which can cause tooth decay. Although certain juices, such as orange, are high in nutrients such as vitamin C, it is better to seek out these nutrients through the whole fruit. Fruit juices are quickly absorbed and cut appetite immediately. If you want your child to be hungry for meals, avoid juice boxes or smoothies made with a base of fruit juice.

If you're looking to feed your baby nutrients through a straw, opt for homemade smoothies and blend the whole fruit rather than adding juice. Whole fruits have less sugar. Smoothies pack an efficient nutritional punch, but consider the ingredients carefully. When making your own smoothies, aim to include twice as many vegetables and proteins as fruit.

The thicker the smoothie, the harder it will be for your child to suck through a straw. Speech therapists use straws to build mouth muscles for talking and for eating. If you've ever sucked a thick milkshake through a straw, you know how much effort it takes. We aren't recommending milkshakes every day, but a power-packed, thick smoothie or even yogurt through a straw is useful every now and then to boost mouth development. If your smoothie is too thick, you can water it down a bit.

> AVOID OFFERING FIZZY DRINKS TO YOUR CHILD. THEY ARE ACIDIC AND SUGAR-LADEN AND CAN DAMAGE TOOTH ENAMEL.

SUGARY DRINKS

Sweetened beverages such as chocolate milk, fruit-flavored drinks, and sugary fizzy drinks are not suitable for young babies and should be strictly limited in children of all ages. These drinks contain sugar and can cause tooth decay even when diluted. They can also lead to poor appetite, weight gain, constipation, and diarrhea.

Drinks that have artificial sweeteners are even worse than sugared beverages because they have potential health implications and can encourage children to develop an inclination for sweets. Even though they may not contain calories, artificially sweetened drink consumption can lead to overeating and weight gain, because they change the way your body responds to food.

Weaning Basics

- Breastfeeding can have a positive effect on your child's IQ and brain development, overall health, the way your child will adapt to her first foods, and her ability to maintain a healthy weight later in life.

- Because the taste of breast milk varies day to day, it can help your child be more accepting of different first food tastes.

- Formula-fed babies who move directly to a brief period of exclusive purees and then to early self-feeding tend to do very well in terms of self-regulation and eating a variety of healthy foods later in life.

- Six months is the ideal time to introduce solids as a complement to breast milk or formula.

- Ideally, you should continue to breast-feed until your baby is around one year, letting feedings decrease organically.

- For the first two or three months of eating solid foods, most of your baby's nutrition will continue to come from breast milk or formula.

- By one year of age your baby's diet should consist of about 24 ounces (710 ml) of breast milk and three meals, with perhaps two small, healthy snacks.

- You'll experience the most success introducing solids when your child is alert and not overly hungry or full.

- Do not feed your baby breast milk or formula and solids at the same feeding.

- Watch for the same hunger cues that you used when you were breastfeeding to decide when to feed.

- It's better to avoid transitioning to a bottle after six months and go right to an open cup or a cup with a straw.

- Skip the lidded cup (or sippy cup). They can lead to dental problems and mouth development issues down the road.

- Try using a straw with a lid on the cup. It helps develop a mature swallow pattern and is less messy than an open cup.

- If your baby is still receiving some breast milk and is eating a wide variety of foods, you can add cow or goat's milk as a supplementary drink after six months of age.

- Avoid or limit sweet or sugary beverages.

CHAPTER 4

Mindful Purees

> "A GOAL IN FOOD INTRODUCTION IS TO FIND OUT WHAT YOUR BABY *LOVES*. I USUALLY RECOMMEND A COMBINATION IN A CO-FEEDING APPROACH USING BOTH [PUREES AND SELF-FEEDING] AND THEN FOLLOW YOUR BABY'S LEAD."
>
> —Marsha Dunn Klein, M.Ed., OTR/L, founder of Mealtime Connections, LLC

So you've determined that your baby is ready to begin exploring solid foods. She is about six months of age and is able to sit with little or no help. Chances are she's also shown an interest in food and may have even tried to grab some food off your plate. This chapter offers advice and tips for getting your eager little baby started on solid foods with purees and eating in a mindful way.

Mindful eating is about being aware of all the foods that you eat and the impact—both positive and negative—that they can have on your body. It's about using

Children Must Sit with Ease Prior to Self-Feeding

The emergence of independent sitting is one of the first major milestones of motor development. It usually occurs around five months of age. By six months of age most children can sit with ease, making it an ideal age to start self-feeding.

all five senses—sight, touch, taste, smell, and sound—to explore foods. When purees are spoon-fed to your child in the traditional manner of a parent leading the spoon to the child's mouth, it focuses primarily on taste and eliminates many aspects of touch except in the mouth. By being mindful of the ways purees are fed, and talking about the smell and even the sound, you can make your child more aware of the foods she eats from a very young age. This mindfulness from an early stage of life will help make your child more aware of the difference between physical hunger and a desire for taste, and help enable her to listen to her satiety cues. Young mindful eaters grow up to be young adults with the tools to make healthy food choices.

Swallowing 101

Before discussing the feeding process in detail, it's important to understand the swallowing process. In addition to sitting and grasping skills, your baby needs to have suitable oral motor function in order to successfully eat whole pieces of food. While infants of six months of age are perfectly capable of mouthing whole foods held in their tiny fist, they need to learn the complex skill of biting and then smashing the food against the roof of their mouth or their gums with their tongues. Then, they learn to keep the smushed food (termed a "bolus") on their tongue and

The Three Phases of Swallowing

Swallowing has three phases and begins during the oral phase:

1 Food enters the mouth, you break down food by chewing, and you push the food with your tongue toward the throat.

2 The pharyngeal phase occurs once you've started to swallow the food. The second phase is about protecting the airway so that food and/or liquid do not enter the lungs.

3 The final phase is the esophageal phase. If you've ever experienced the feeling of food being stuck deep in your throat, that's an esophageal phase dysfunction. Swallowing is deceptively complicated; it involves at least 34 pairs of muscles before food lands in the belly.

propel it backward to be swallowed. That's challenging, because babies at this age have a natural forward-backward tongue movement that tends to push food out, rather than keeping it in the mouth. As food moves toward the back of the mouth, the body's first protective response is to gag. It takes time to learn to tolerate new tastes, temperatures, and textures. Eventually, gagging will occur less frequently and babies will become better at swallowing food rather than spitting it out.

Introduce Purees First

From a developmental perspective, purees can be helpful for the baby. When a child learns to suckle from the breast or bottle, she forms a vacuum around her mouth. This intra-oral pressure drives the milk into the baby's mouth and down her throat. When a baby is ready to move to solid foods, she needs to change the way she gets food into her mouth. Purees help teach proper swallowing technique, that is, propelling foods backward with the tongue and swallowing. Babies are less prone to gag or choke on purees than on solids.

Strict advocates of baby-led weaning, however, recommend total avoidance of purees. Baby-led weaning changes the order in which children learn to eat. With a puree, babies learn to swallow first and then chew. With baby-led weaning, the thought is that babies learn to chew first and swallowing comes later. Specialists in mouth development will argue this, but in any case, until a baby learns to swallow, she will chew on her food and either spit it out or gag on it as she tries to get it down her throat.

Advocates of baby-led weaning are quick to point out that there is a difference between gagging and choking, and that a baby must learn to gag productively. This may be true for some children who have the motor skills to manage solid foods. However, struggling with solids foods before your baby has mastered the basics of swallowing can cause unnecessary stress on both the caregivers and the child. Not every parent is able to calmly stand by while his baby experiences gagging. The experience is uncomfortable, regardless of whether your baby is in immediate danger or not. The experience is not pleasant for babies, either. If a child gags excessively and struggles with her first foods, she may vomit and can develop a negative association with eating, which can have a lasting impact on the way she interacts with food. Gagging can also exacerbate gastroesophageal reflux, where stomach contents rise up into the baby's throat. It makes sense to help your baby become comfortable with the basics of swallowing by introducing purees, before she tackles chunks of food held in her fists.

Likewise, many feeding professionals who are certified speech-language pathologists or registered occupational therapists trained in the developmental process of feeding have concerns about skipping purees entirely. "Purees help intrinsic tongue muscles develop, preparing them to chew and swallow more efficiently," says Catherine Shaker, M.S., CCC-SLP, a swallowing specialist.

Child health specialist Charlotte M. Wright found in a 2011 University of Glasgow study that while avoiding purees works for some babies, it could lead to nutritional problems for children who develop more slowly than others. Wright concluded, "It is more realistic to encourage infants to self-feed with solid finger food during family meals, but also give them spoon-fed purees."

If your baby struggles with solid finger foods, don't rush him past this crucial step in the developmental process. If he's swallowing purees comfortably yet only mouthing and spitting out the self-feeding foods, allow him to keep exploring both textures. With time, he'll master both. Also, there are times when feeding finger foods is especially challenging—such as when your baby is ill or you want to avoid a mess while dining out. There are mindful ways to use purees while still working to develop your baby's development and nutrition.

Even once your child has started to self-feed you should continue to offer the spoon with purees at least three times per week. Kids need continued exposure to a variety of foods in order to keep them in their repertoire. Green bean puree today leads to green bean casserole in the future. Plus, continued exposure to parental spoon-feeding will make self-spoon feeding that much easier in the near future. Just as important, the texture of purees is an important and necessary experience for your baby's sensory system to process consistent information about food. Puree feeding can be a loving, reciprocal experience for both baby and parents or caregivers. Feeding our children is based on a nurturing, responsive relationship. Both purees and self-feeding foods require a partnership where we are enjoying each other's company while also enjoying our food.

The Role of Early Spoon-Feeding

Spoon-feeding your baby purees plays a specific, useful role. Babies develop better lip control and movement as they suck a puree off a spoon. It also limits the amount of food your baby will spit out and gets more food into your baby's tummy. However, most parents place the spoon in their child's mouth and then scrape the food off on the top of their baby's lip as they remove the spoon. Instead, you can teach your baby to suck the food off the spoon.

PROPER SPOON-FEEDING TECHNIQUES

Teaching your baby to suck food off a spoon the correct way helps to position her tongue in the proper place in order to push food toward her throat.

1. Get down on eye level with your baby. Do not feed your baby while you are standing above her. When a baby has to look up at you, it makes it more difficult for her to swallow comfortably. Plus, you'll tend to lift the spoon upward.

2. Start with the tip of the spoon dipped in the puree. Think of first tastes as just that—a taste. Gradually work up to a spoonful.

3. Bring the spoon toward your baby's mouth, waiting for him to open and accept the spoon. Reading your baby's cues is essential. You are building a nurturing relationship where the shared experience of feeding is the foundation. Resist the urge to scrape the food off on your baby's upper lip or the roof of his mouth. Allow him to close his top lip and suck the puree off the spoon while you guide the spoon straight out of his mouth in tandem. Keeping the spoon parallel to the floor helps your baby develop the proper tongue position for the next phase, swallowing.

4. Allow time for your baby to propel the puree backward and swallow. This typically takes a second or two, but at first you'll notice baby pushing the food back out and then swallowing. With time, this suckle reflex (a forward/backward motion) will begin to fade and she will eventually swallow more food than she pushes out.

5. Repeat. Remember to read your baby's cues, smile, and talk to him. Eating is a social experience. You'll know your baby is eager to participate if he:

- Opens his mouth as the spoon approaches.
- Leans forward slightly to accept the spoon.
- Has a pleasant expression on his face.
- Gazes at you while you are feeding.
- Grabs at the spoon to bring it to his mouth on his own or with your help.

6. If baby closes her mouth, becomes fussy, or is otherwise resistant to eating, don't force it. Put the food away and feed with breast milk or formula. Then try puree again in another day or two. Watch for signs that your baby is not ready to be fed:

- Turns away from the spoon
- Closes mouth when spoon approaches
- Gags
- Gazes away from the spoon
- Blocks spoon with hands or covers mouth with hands

The Benefits of Starting with Purees

- **Reduces gagging and discomfort for baby.**
- **Increases chance of having a positive first experience with food.**
- **Helps teach your baby proper swallowing technique.**
- **Introduces your child to the texture of pureed food.**

FEEDING OUR CHILDREN IS BASED ON A NURTURING, RESPONSIVE RELATIONSHIP. BOTH PUREES AND SELF-FEEDING FOODS REQUIRE A PARTNERSHIP WHERE WE ARE ENJOYING EACH OTHER'S COMPANY WHILE ALSO ENJOYING OUR FOOD.

CHOOSING THE RIGHT SPOON

A spoon is simply a tool to present purees. Many parents in countries around the world use their finger, a piece of solid food dipped in puree, or even baby's own hands as the first tool for presenting "suckable" foods. For the purposes of this book, we suggest a spoon, with the understanding that it's the act of sucking the puree that is most important.

Parents often feed babies with adult-size spoons or toddler spoons, when in fact the first spoon should be very flat with a small "spoon-bowl." Babies have small mouths and need small spoons for comfort and for learning how to suck food off a spoon. Choose a spoon that has a flat, narrow bowl just big enough to fit over your baby's tongue, but not cover the edges of the tongue. Your child needs to be able to lift the sides (lateral margins) of her tongue upward just slightly as the spoon rests on her tongue, then close her top lip and clean the food off the spoon as you draw it out of her mouth. Learning to use the lateral margins of the tongue and the lips (especially the top lip) helps a child develop a mature swallow pattern for chewing and swallowing more advanced textures with ease.

Early spoon skills lead to ease with early straw drinking, which we will discuss in the chapter on emergent eaters.

The Transition to Self-Spoon-Feeding

The secret to getting the most out of self-feeding is to know when to move on from exclusive purees. Most babies can start to self-feed by seven months. Although you can continue to offer purees occasionally, they should no longer make up a large part of your baby's diet after seven or eight months of age. A baby who gets too used to a certain way of eating can become reluctant to try new tastes and textures. He will also miss out on the learning

"SOME BABIES WILL HAVE GREAT DIFFICULTY LEARNING TO ACCEPT SOLID FOOD IF NOT STARTED BEFORE SEVEN TO NINE MONTHS OF AGE."

—Dr. Jack Newman

experience of feeding himself at a young age. Once your baby can competently swallow purees, it's time to introduce self-spoon-feeding and finger foods.

Babies will begin dipping with a spoon around nine months of age. The next step is scooping, which may emerge a few months later. Parents can keep offering spoonfuls of purees and mashed foods to their babies until about 12 months of age. Offering a spoon occasionally during this time period exposes children to a variety of tastes and textures while they learn to manage the dipping, and later scooping, stages on their own. Mastering messy, self-spoon-feeding may not happen until about 15 to 18 months.

FEEDING FREQUENCY

In the beginning, perhaps during the first few weeks of introducing solids, offer purees twice a day. Ideally, you should feed at the same time that other family members are eating. For example, you could all eat breakfast together, continue to feed your baby breast milk or formula during the day, and eat together as a family for dinner. Or you could feed purees at breakfast and lunch and then skip dinner. Consider what works best for your family's schedule.

Don't be overly concerned with how much puree your baby is eating or in what order vegetables are being introduced. During this time the majority of your baby's calories and nutrients will continue to come from breast milk or formula. Still, there are many reasons for introducing purees:

- To teach baby to enjoy the taste, temperature, and texture of new foods
- To teach baby the next steps in managing solids for swallowing
- To introduce the concept of family mealtime
- To share how much fun eating healthy food can be

Remember, offering a baby purees contributes to the shared experience of mealtimes and the development of the mouth and oral motor skills. Just like learning to crawl, walk, and run, feeding is a developmental process!

Expose Your Child to Veggies First

Vegetables are a crucial yet underrepresented part of most children's diets. Most children ages 5 to 15 eat just one portion of vegetables a day, and 7 percent of children don't eat any vegetables at all. Since nutritional interventions later in life are difficult to implement, and largely unsuccessful, more and more experts are encouraging parents to take early steps to ensure that their children accept vegetables early and learn to include them in their diet (and even enjoy them).

Experts often recommend that vegetables be your child's first solid food taste. However, some experts are going beyond that recommendation and suggesting that parents introduce the flavor of vegetables prior to giving their child actual solid food. This idea is nearly ingrained in French culture. Since many children generally dislike vegetables, it has become a common cultural practice in France to expose vegetables as a first food by adding a small amount of vegetable puree or vegetable cooking water to the infant's milk just prior to weaning them to solids.

Breastfed infants are naturally exposed to flavor variations in breast milk, due to the variety of dietary flavors transmitted through the mother's breast milk. This process is known as a flavor bridge. That being said, breast milk still tends to be very sweet, regardless of what the mother has had to eat. French mothers suggest that by altering the flavor bridge—adding vegetables to either breast milk or formula—you can make infants more willing to eat vegetables when you move them to solid foods.

This has been borne out in research. A University of Leeds study, for example, looked at 36 mothers and split them into two groups. One group gave their babies plain breast milk or formula for 12 consecutive days followed by plain rice cereal for 12 consecutive days. The other group gave their babies breast milk or formula with a little vegetable puree added for 12 consecutive days, followed by rice cereal with vegetable puree added for 12 days. Immediately following these 24-day periods, the babies in each group were given vegetable puree for 11 consecutive days. The vegetables were given in a rotation of carrots, green beans, spinach, and broccoli.

The group of babies who had originally been given vegetable puree in their milk and cereal ate 46 percent more vegetable puree than the group who had received rice cereal as their first solid food tastes without any vegetables added. The babies who had been gradually weaned onto vegetables also consumed the vegetable purees at a faster rate and showed a greater liking for vegetables when researchers revisited the babies six months later.

Vegetables tend to be bitter. Gradually introducing them helps children get used to the taste and understand that these are, in fact, helpful, not harmful, foods. It appears that doing a relatively simple thing, like adding vegetable puree to milk or baby cereal can encourage children to eat vegetables more readily when solid foods are introduced.

Regardless of whether or not you decided to introduce the taste of vegetables through your baby's breast milk or formula, we recommend that vegetables be among your baby's first tastes. You can vary the texture of vegetable purees by mixing them with a bit of oatmeal, wheat, or barley cereal; however, baby cereals are not always necessary, and rice cereal should be avoided on a regular basis (more on this below).

Limit Rice Products

Has anyone ever told you to put your cell phone in a bag of rice if you drop the phone in water? This is because rice is naturally absorbent. Rice also absorbs toxins, such as arsenic, regardless of whether the rice is grown under conventional or organic farming practices. Arsenic is found naturally in soil and water and is absorbed more readily into rice than other grains and produce. All rice products, including rice cereal, contain some level of arsenic, which can be harmful in large amounts.

While adults and older children are more fully equipped to eliminate these toxins from the body, even small amounts of arsenic can be harmful to an infant. Arsenic can build up over time, and high levels of arsenic are associated with higher rates of skin, bladder, and lung cancers.

With so many other food options, it's best to limit rice cereal. The American Academy of Pediatrics advises that parents offer their children a wide variety of foods to reduce exposure to arsenic from rice. Once you start self-feeding, it shouldn't be harmful for your baby to eat rice products on occasion. It is difficult to avoid entirely. However, it should be offered only on occasion and not as a daily food staple for at least the first year.

The Long-Term Effects of Early Nutrition

Early nutrition has profound implications for the long-term health of your child. The right food choices can help boost cognitive function, encourage healthy growth patterns, reduce the risk of obesity, and decrease the risk of cardiovascular disease and cancer later in life.

Incorporate Fruit

It wasn't long ago that doctors recommended waiting for three days in between introducing new foods out of fear of an allergic reaction. These days this stance is not so strict. The allergy risk from introducing most types of produce is quite low. You may feed your baby one type of puree at breakfast and another at dinner, or begin to offer a few different tastes at one meal. This is a perfect time to introduce fruits, either alongside the vegetable being offered or alternating between the two.

It's always preferable to choose organic produce whenever possible to reduce your child's exposure to pesticides. We encourage you to make your own purees if you'd like to, but don't get overly concerned if you don't have the time and need to rely on store-bought baby food. As soon as your baby is comfortable swallowing purees from a spoon, it's time to transition to self-feeding for most of your baby's eating experiences.

Readily available fruits that are easy to handle in little hands and little mouths are:

- Avocado (Surprised? It's actually a fruit or a large berry thanks to the seed tucked inside!)
- Pears, ripe and soft with all skin removed
- Apples of all varieties, roasted or baked with skin removed

Limit Acidic Fruits

Although most fruits are fine for babies, citrus and acidic fruits, such as pineapples and oranges, may cause rashes and upset the digestive system due to their high acidity. Limit them to small doses, such as adding lemon juice to a puree, for the first few months of feeding.

Are Purees Always Necessary?

Purees will be a part of most babies' early food experiences, but that doesn't mean they are absolutely necessary for every baby. Spoon-feeding your baby plays a role in easing the transition from liquids to self-feeding. If your child is resistant to purees, remember that your goal is to offer variety and let your child explore. Continue to offer purees once or twice a day for a week or two. Then wait and go back to them in another few weeks. Don't be overly upset if she continues to turn her nose up at them.

Some babies will be able to learn to swallow very easily and can transition to finger foods effectively with minimal gagging. If your baby repeatedly refuses purees, offer him an appropriately soft piece of food. If he doesn't have trouble swallowing, you can move to self-feeding. If your baby has trouble with the soft foods and seems to gag a lot or spit them out, stick with breast milk or formula and continue to offer purees for a few more weeks. If purees still haven't caught on, try self-feeding again.

Once you move to finger foods, continue to offer purees occasionally to expose your baby to that texture. A baby who initially rejected purees on a spoon may be more willing to try them a few months later through a straw or baby-led-spoon-feeding.

As long as your baby is happy and gaining weight as expected, you don't need to worry about the exact types or order of foods or method of feeding. Feeding your baby should be engaging and fun—do what you can to avoid stressing over the exact timeline and methods.

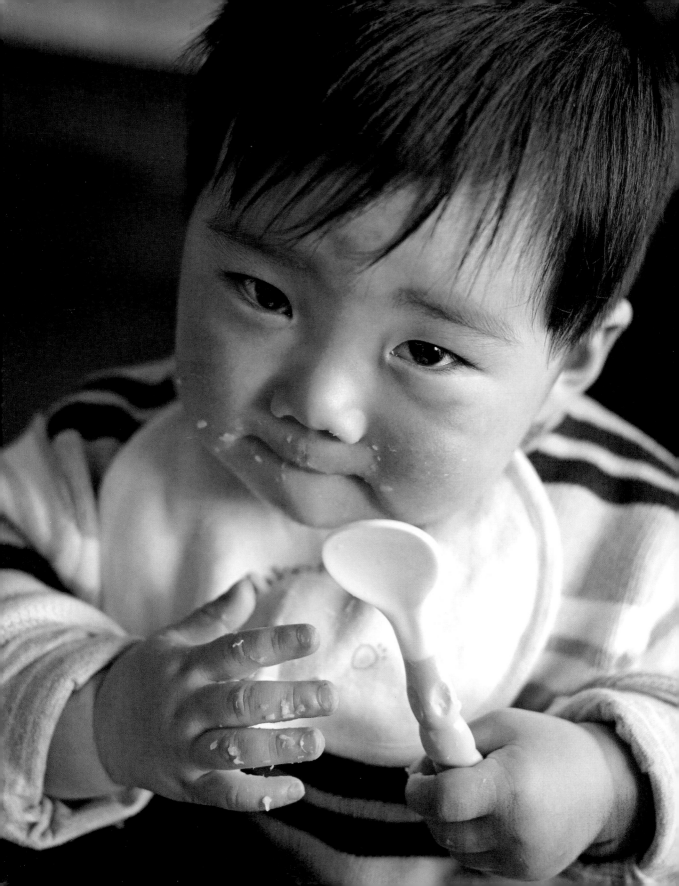

CHAPTER 5

A Healthy Start with Self-Feeding

Throughout the feeding process it is important to follow your baby's cues. Babies develop at different rates, and while one child may be ready to start eating handheld and finger foods at six months, another might not until eight months. Before you start adding handheld and finger foods to your baby's diet, she should:

1. Be able to remain in a seated position while holding her head steady. Your baby may be able to sit in a high chair on her own or in an assisted seated position with rolled-up towels. Your baby needs to be upright without the fear of toppling over to one side. It's hard to eat when you're slumped over!

2. Have basic hand, eye, and mouth coordination so that she is able to look at food and pick it up and put it in her mouth.

Nix the Bumbo

Feeding therapists are not big fans of Bumbo chairs. They put early feeders into a posterior pelvic tilt that increases pressure on the lower esophageal sphincter, causing baby to reflux. For a few kids, Bumbos can be helpful (even feeding therapists make exceptions to a rule), but most fare better without them, due to the poor positioning they cause. It's better to wait until your baby can sit independently.

3. Be able to swallow purees. If your baby can't propel the purees back and swallow with ease, she'll be less likely to adjust comfortably to self-feeding. Prior to introducing self-feeding, try to feed your baby her first purees. This exclusive puree phase will be a short but essential part of the feeding process, which will bridge sucking liquids to sucking purees off a spoon to sucking small pieces of soft foods that have loosened as your child mouths self-feeding foods.

A baby who cannot manage the bolus of purees or soft finger foods will either spit her solid food back out, gag, or both. Some babies will not like purees—every baby is different. If your child refuses purees after repeated tries you may want to try moving directly to fingers foods.

Grasping Food by the Numbers

Sixty-eight percent of children can grasp food with their hands by 6 months, 85 percent of children can grasp food with their hands by 7 months, and 96 percent of children can grasp food with their hands by 8 months.

Regardless of what you are feeding your baby, you need to remember to proceed slowly. Babies need time and patience to figure out the feeding process, and some need a longer "bridge" to success than others. Don't be concerned or ashamed if your baby takes longer to reach this stage. Babies' bodies need to develop (muscles, coordination, etc.), and this happens at different rates. It is not necessarily reflective of a slow learning process.

What You'll Need to Introduce Self-Feeding

Once your baby is comfortable swallowing purees it's time to introduce finger foods. For most babies this will be around seven months of age, but don't worry if your baby takes a little longer. Your goal in self-feeding is to let your baby take part in directing his eating habits—let him also take part in deciding when he's ready.

Self-Feeding Checklist

☐ Can your baby remain in a seated position while holding her head steady?

☐ Does your baby have age-appropriate hand, eye, and mouth coordination?

☐ Can she look at food, pick it up, and put it in her mouth with relatively little struggle?

☐ Is your baby able to swallow food comfortably?

☐ Is your baby a full-term, healthy baby?

At first your infant will make a munching motion when exploring handheld finger foods, using up-and-down movements of the jaw to break up food. Also, by about six months of age, your baby will begin to demonstrate emerging skill with tongue lateralization, in order to move food around inside his mouth and take food to the back of his mouth for swallowing. Because he's already started sucking purees off of a spoon, he's had enhanced lessons in propelling food backward for swallowing. Once your baby has these feeding skills, it is important to put them to immediate use.

Infants exposed to finger foods after nine months of age are more likely to have feeding difficulties and to be picky eaters. Studies have found that children who are introduced to "lumpy" foods after nine months of age have more feeding difficulties, more definite likes and dislikes, and a more restricted diet at seven years of age compared to children who were introduced to finger foods between six and eight months of age.

The most important thing is to remember to keep things light and enjoyable. Learning to self-feed should be a fun experience for you and your baby. You want your baby's first experience with exploring new flavors and textures on her own to be positive. Try not to be overly concerned with the mess and how much food is actually being consumed. In the first few months of self-feeding, how much your baby ingests is less important than getting her used to the idea of exploring and eating new foods.

Who needs a plate?
An all-in-one suction
mat makes
mealtime simple.

SKIP THE PLATE

Self-feeding doesn't require a lot of equipment. Your baby will be eating most of the same foods that you do, so you don't need anything special to prepare his meals. Don't worry about putting food on a plate. It's a baby's natural instinct to pick up anything in front of him, and that includes a bowl or plate! Once it lands on the floor, the "throw the plate" game often becomes a mealtime distraction. Instead, put the food directly on the high chair tray or preferably on the tabletop. Another option is a place mat and partitioned plate all in one that sticks to the tabletop and is practically impossible for a baby to toss. We love the ezpz mat (shown here), which was designed just for the purpose of containing the mess and solves the problem of plate tossing.

THE ANATOMY OF THE PERFECT HIGH CHAIR

Finding the right high chair takes some research. Here are some elements to look for.

- Make sure that you choose one that is easy to clean and wipe down. It should also have minimal crevices for food to get stuck in. If there's a cushion, look at how it fits with the frame and see if there are any gaps or spaces for food. If you can't wipe a high chair down after a feeding, you don't want it.

- You also want to inspect the safety harness to make sure it is adequate to keep your child seated in place once she gets older and can move around. Once again, the harness should be easy to clean.

- It should have a removable tray. You can choose a freestanding high chair or a hook-on portable chair, provided that it offers effective trunk support. The latter is a great choice if you are short on space or if you dine out a lot because you can bring it with you to snap onto restaurant tables.

- Make sure it's at the right height for your table and so that baby's elbows can rest on the table or tray.

No matter which chair you choose, remember that a baby needs support around his hips and often his trunk, especially when he is first learning to eat. Try rolling up a bath towel and then wrapping it around your baby's hips to fill in the space between the chair and his hips and bottom. Your baby's pelvis should tilt forward slightly, just like an adult sitting on a bar stool with no backrest. The anterior pelvic tilt puts his trunk into an ideal upright position with the shoulders positioned directly over the hips. Position the hips correctly and support the trunk, and eating will be so much easier!

Before you start your baby self-feeding, decide where she will be eating. While purees can be spoon-fed to a baby who is sitting upright in any safe location—even on another adult's lap—self-feeding requires a bit more thought. It's going to be messy, sometimes really messy. It pays to spend a little advance time planning your baby's primary eating area.

If possible, place the high chair on tile, hardwood, or an easy-to-clean surface. If you have to place the high chair on carpet, make sure there is a large piece of plastic or a tablecloth under the high chair so you can wipe it down easily after a meal. If it's nice outside, why not consider doing mealtime outdoors? You can set up a spot in the shade, take off baby's shirt, and let her go nuts.

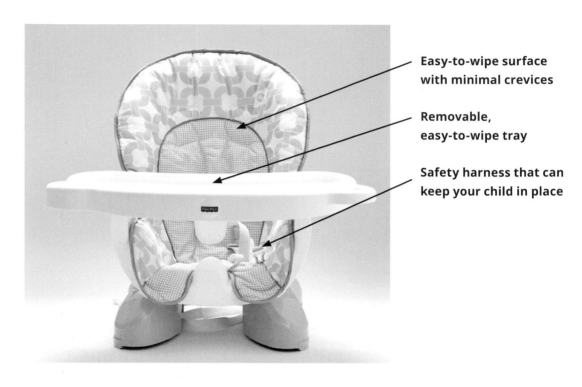

Easy-to-wipe surface with minimal crevices

Removable, easy-to-wipe tray

Safety harness that can keep your child in place

Upright, supportive seating

Elbows on the table or tray

Highchair Recommendations

- The **Boon Pedestal** high chair is one of Nancy's favorites. Not only is the modern design fab, but it's also easy to clean. The one-piece seat has no cracks or crevices, making it a breeze to clean up. The tray cover is dishwasher safe and pops off and fits in your dishwasher. It also has continuous height positioning with a pneumatic lift so you can get the high chair at the perfect height for your table. (www.booninc.com/index.php)

- Melanie loves any chair that is adjustable as a child grows, including the wooden **Stokke Tripp Trapp** or the less expensive **Keekaroo Height Right**, which has accessories like an infant seat for added support. Although both chairs are slightly more money than the standard plastic high chair, the seat and footrests are easily adjustable and the chairs grow with the child into school age. (www.stokke.com, www.keekaroo.com)

- For babies, try the very inexpensive **Fisher-Price Spacesaver**. It positions a child beautifully for all types of feeding experiences, from purees to self-feeding. It's ideal for infants through nine months of age, when they are ready to transition to the other chairs noted here. Smaller babies can stay in the Spacesaver for a few months longer too. (www.fisher-price.com)

- Prefer a hook-on chair? **Phil&Teds Lobster** hook-on chair tops the list in function and design. The stainless steel frame is firm, is easy to carry, and can be clamped onto almost any table. Padded shoulder straps keep your child safely in the chair, and a removable plastic tray provides a clean and safe area for baby to eat. Plus, it provides a flat seat rather than the common parachute or soft cloth under your baby's bottom. Think about eating while seated in a hammock—it's not easy! (www.philandteds.com)

BIBS

We love kids to get messy! Experiencing food through the multitude of nerve endings in their hands and fingers prepares babies for what they are about to encounter when the food enters their mouths. Did you know there are even more sensitive nerves in the mouth? In a perfect world, we'd prefer you just slip off your baby's shirt and let him experience food on the most basic level. Of course, that's not always possible, so unless you want to go through multiple outfits a day, you'll need a quality bib.

For less mess, bigger is better. Try to cover as much surface area as possible with your bib. There are bibs with sleeves that fit on like an extra layer of clothing. If your baby is happy wearing one of these, they're a helpful choice because "body bibs" can save you having to change your child's clothing after each meal.

Designer Bibs

Mally Designs has an online custom bib studio (mallydesigns.com/custom) that lets you change the color and design of your child's bib and even add his name. The leather bibs are easy to wipe clean and are so long lasting that they may well be the only bib your child will need.

Another inexpensive option is to make your own body bib out of a large T-shirt. Take a T-shirt that is a bit too big for your child, either with long or short sleeves. Simply cut up the back from the bottom to the neckline. Next, cut away a strip of cloth on either side of the original center cut (about 6 inches [15 cm] wide), again from the bottom to the neckline, but stop just before cutting into the crew of the neck. Those long strips are your ties to secure the bib—trim them as needed. Make a dozen of these T-shirt bibs and you'll have a soft, comfortable bib that completely covers your child's clothes and can be tossed right into the washer. If you're talented with a sewing machine, add a colorful ribbon along all the edges, too!

Lastly, you may decide to opt for one or two quality wipeable bibs with a surface such as plastic, laminated canvas, or even leather. You can just wipe them down after mealtime and they're ready for the next food encounter.

Establish a Feeding Schedule

Babies have small stomachs. When you first introduce solid foods they will continue to follow a pattern of multiple daily feedings rather than three structured meals. In the beginning, the multiple feedings will be a combination of solid food and breast milk or formula.

Start by deciding on two solid food mealtimes that work best for your family. Consider your child's sleep pattern, taking into account naps. A lot of parents find that it works best to offer their baby the breast immediately upon waking and then wait about 30 to 60 minutes before offering their baby her first solid meal. You can then choose between a lunch or a dinner feeding depending on which is more convenient for your family.

You don't need to stick with the exact same feeding times every day, but try to be as consistent as possible—babies thrive on a schedule—and feed your baby with the rest of the family whenever you can. It'll make it easier for everyone if your baby is eating when everyone else does. You want your young child to be part of the family mealtime from the start. If you have a day when feeding with everyone else is not possible, one parent might have a snack while feeding the infant so that she is still partaking in the food experience with someone else.

Once your baby gets used to eating solid food, you will find that breastfeeding and formula sessions will gradually be replaced with a meal or snack. Work your way up to three family meals by 8 to 10 months of age, depending on your baby's temperament and appetite. By about one year your baby will be eating three family meals and one or two small snacks.

Sample Feeding Schedule

6:30 a.m. Breast milk or formula feeding upon waking

7:30 a.m. Family breakfast

9:30 a.m. Nap time (optional breastfeeding prior to nap)

11:30 a.m. Lunch with family

1:00 p.m. Breastfeeding or formula prior to nap

3:30 p.m. Breast milk or formula feeding

6:30 p.m. Breast milk or formula feeding before bed

The Joy (and Importance) of Getting Messy

One of the eventualities of self-feeding is the mess. Kids are sensory learners and they're programed to explore. There are a lot of nerve endings in their palms and fingertips. These give signals back to the brain to help your child identify, use, and learn via tactile sensations.

Notice how your baby plays with toys once he is able to pick things up. He will grab a toy and bring it to the midline and then to his mouth. This is an attempt to learn about feeding and to learn what goes into his mouth and what should not. Kids who do not explore with their hands when they eat can find feeding time very overwhelming. They are missing the opportunity to learn and explore what goes into their mouths.

Of course, parents don't always want mealtime to be a disaster. If you're going to a friend's house for dinner or out to a restaurant, you don't want your little one to be covered head to toe in spaghetti and meatballs. You can use purees for convenience on occasion if your child will take them. If not, choose less messy foods such as steamed carrots or broccoli on occasions when you just cannot bear the mess. But if it's bath time after dinner anyway, then go nuts and let your baby explore and have fun!

It's easy to get overwhelmed with all the do's and don'ts of feeding your baby for the first time, but don't forget to make mealtime fun. Teach your child from an early age about the importance of family mealtime. When possible, let your child explore and have fun with her food. Try not to get overly concerned with the mess and know that this stage is a short (but important) period in her life. Enjoy the learning process with her.

Mindful Eating

How many well-intentioned parents have turned eating purees into a game by turning a loaded spoon into an airplane? As the carrot puree dips and turns across the table aided by parental sound effects, the child is expected to gleefully open up her mouth and let the cargo land. Take a second to think about the message this air show is sending to your child. It's making mealtime playtime.

If your child is already a hesitant eater it can actually reinforce the behavior of not eating. The parent's "air show" is exciting for the baby, but when he opens his mouth for food, the show ends. If he refuses to open his mouth, he is entertained longer while the parent tries harder to get the plane on the landing strip. For hesitant and eager eaters, the air show conditions the baby to learn that food should come with entertainment. Instead of creating so many distractions, which can lead to mindless eating, focus on the joy of being together. Your smile and delighted facial expressions and your eye-to-eye conversations during mealtimes are all the reinforcement a baby needs.

Instead of directing the food experience for your child, let your child lead the experience. Your child should be guided by his five senses—sight, sound, touch, smell, and, of course, taste. It's all right for children to get messy and have some fun with their food. However, it should be self-directed. Let your child touch and explore his food, and bring it up to his nose to smell it. Using the five senses is a huge part of becoming a mindful eater, and becoming aware of the foods that are put in your mouth.

> USING THE FIVE SENSES IS A HUGE PART OF BECOMING A MINDFUL EATER, AND BECOMING AWARE OF THE FOODS THAT ARE PUT IN YOUR MOUTH.

Exceptions to Early Self-Feeding

There is a growing population of kids who have difficulties learning to eat, especially young babies. In fact, the number is much larger than it was 20 years ago. Although experts aren't exactly sure why this number is growing, one reason could be the growing number of viable premature births. Feeding difficulties are present in 25 percent of children and in up to 80 percent of children with developmental disabilities.

Nearly 500,000 babies are born prematurely in the United States each year. Any baby born prior to 37 weeks is considered premature. Not only is the number of premature births on the rise, but so is the survival rates of these babies.

While some preemies go on to thrive without any lasting complications, there can be a variety of challenges in the first several years of life. When a child is born prematurely, her sensory system does not develop at the same speed as a baby born on schedule. The mouth has more sensory receptors per square inch than any other part of the body, making feeding issues among the most common problems preemies have. Preemies need to take extra care in learning to eat and will likely not be ready for finger foods as early as other babies because their sensory systems and motor development mature at different rates than those of full-term babies.

Preemies may also experience complications such as acid reflux and lung issues that can make feeding difficult. In addition, they may harbor negative feelings from early unpleasant experiences with trying to feed. Caution and time need to be taken when introducing solids to a preemie, and self-feeding should be held off until at least eight or nine months of age, and possibly longer.

Babies who have had any early medical issues can also develop early eating issues. Medical interventions can alter the sensory system, making the feeding experience more intense. Tread lightly when introducing food to a baby who has experienced medical issues, and talk to your doctor prior to attempting self-feeding.

> ONE OUT OF EVERY EIGHT INFANTS BORN IN THE UNITED STATES IS PREMATURE. BECAUSE PREEMIES ARE MORE SENSITIVE TO EXTERNAL STIMULI, THEY CAN HAVE DIFFICULTY LEARNING TO EAT. EARLY SELF-FEEDING MAY NOT BE AN OPTION.

Even if your baby has had early success with self-feeding, you may need to revert to offering only purees if your infant is sick. Babies who are unwell or recuperating may not have the energy or stamina to meet their energy and nutrient requirements through self-feeding. Follow your baby's cues and know that it's okay to go back to purees. Even if your baby is older than nine months, if he is unwell and does not want to self-feed, offer assistance. When he is feeling better, return to self-feeding.

In general, if your baby isn't interested in food the best thing you can do as a parent is to wait patiently and continue to offer food every few days. Follow your baby's cues and feed her when she's responsive. If not, don't make a big deal about it and try again later. If you persist in a calm and loving manner, your child will let you know when she's ready to try her first foods.

If you have any concerns, talk with your child's pediatrician and consult with a professional who is familiar with baby self-feeding techniques to see how you might incorporate or adapt some of the techniques offered in this book.

Self-Feeding Essentials

- Let your baby determine the pace of mealtime and how much he will eat at each feeding.
- As soon as your baby learns to swallow purees, start feeding him the same foods that you eat.
- Cut finger foods into manageable and safe pieces.
- Introducing a variety of healthy foods at an early age helps your child become a more adventurous eater.
- It is okay and even recommended to start with purees and continue them for the first few weeks of solid feeding.
- You can use purees occasionally after the first month for convenience; just don't make them a regular part of your baby's eating regime.
- Kids who do not explore with their hands when they eat can find feeding time overwhelming.
- Let your child get messy and have fun with his food.
- Teach your child from an early age about the importance of family mealtime.

- CHAPTER 6 -
Understanding Your Child's Early Nutritional Needs

In the first year of life your baby will triple her weight and increase the length of her body by 50 percent. This rapid growth and development needs to be backed with sound nutrition to help your baby grow and thrive. "Most of your baby's nutritional needs are met by breast milk or formula in the first year," says Dr. Newman. However, once your baby starts solid foods, around six months of age, you are setting the foundations for a lifetime of healthy eating. By the end of your baby's first year, your child should have the skills to fully support herself by eating solid foods. In this chapter we cover the basics of healthy eating and look at the nutrients your child needs to thrive.

The basic building blocks of food include carbohydrates, protein, and fat. While healthy foods are the same at any age, the nutritional needs of your baby will differ from yours. For example, a baby's diet should consist of 10 to 20 percent more fat than an adult's diet in order to support his rapid growth and ability to metabolize fats at a faster rate.

Carbohydrates

Carbohydrates are your child's primary energy source. Ideally, carbohydrates should make up 50 to 60 percent of your child's diet. Most children get enough carbs in their diet; often the concern is avoiding too many carbs. It's also important that your child eat the right type of carbohydrates. There are two types of carbohydrates: simple and complex.

SIMPLE CARBOHYDRATES

Simple carbohydrates can be natural or refined. Natural carbohydrates, such as fruit, provide a quick energy boost and supply vitamins and minerals, but refined carbohydrates are processed and should be limited. Examples of refined carbohydrates are white flour and sugars; they have little to no nutritional value. Foods that contain high amounts of refined carbohydrates include crackers, breakfast cereals, sweetened yogurts, baked goods, cookies, and candy.

Common Refined Simple Carbohydrates

Limit these refined simple carbohydrates in your child's diet:

- White flour
- White sugar
- Brown sugar
- Corn syrup
- Honey
- Maple syrup
- Molasses
- Jam and jelly
- Sweetened juice
- Candy
- Soda/pop

COMPLEX CARBOHYDRATES

Complex carbohydrates are dietary starches and are made of sugar molecules strung together like a necklace. Your body has to work harder to break them down, so therefore they provide a more continuous source of energy. Complex carbohydrates are usually rich in fiber, vitamins, and nutrients. Sources include vegetables, whole grains, beans, and legumes.

Power Up on Complex Carbohydrates

The majority of your child's food intake should come from a broad spectrum of complex carbohydrates. These include:

- Vegetables
- Whole grains (e.g., oatmeal, whole grain bread, whole grain pasta)
- Beans and lentils

Protein

Protein is fundamental to the architecture of our bodies. The body uses protein to build new cells, maintain and repair tissues, and synthesize new proteins that make it possible to perform basic bodily functions. Protein is essential for muscle growth and development; healthy hair, nails, and skin; and bone development.

While protein is essential to your child's development, young children don't need a lot of it. Just 10 to 20 percent of your child's daily calories should come from protein. Since you are continuing with breast milk or using formula until your baby reaches one year, most of your child's protein needs will be met through those liquids. If your child also eats a little meat, beans, eggs, or fish, she will have easily met her protein requirements. Don't worry if your child isn't eating much. Even half an ounce of daily protein in addition to breast milk and formula will meet the minimum requirements. Once your child reaches one year of age he will need about 16 grams of protein a day, which can be met by 2 cups (470 ml) of whole milk and about 1 ounce (28 g) of beef or fish.

Top 10 Protein-Rich Foods for Your Baby

Here's a look at the protein count in these popular self-feeding choices for your baby:

1 ounce (28 g) pork tenderloin	7 grams
1 ounce (28 g) beef tenderloin	6.5 grams
1 ounce (28 g) salmon	6 grams
1 egg	6 grams
¼ cup (60 g) tofu	5 grams
1 ounce (28 g) ground beef	4 grams
1 tablespoon (15 g) black beans	2.5 grams
¼ cup (30 g) quinoa, cooked	2 grams
⅓ cup (30 g) oatmeal, cooked	2 grams
1 ounce (28 g) plain yogurt	1 gram

Your baby's diet should include 50 to 60 percent carbohydrates, 30 to 40 percent fat, and 10 to 20 percent protein.

Fat

Fats are an important part of your child's diet. They are an important energy source for growing bodies, help your child's body absorb fat-soluble vitamins, and are essential for proper development. Because they are growing so rapidly, young children require more fat than older children or adults do. Children under the age of 4 should get 30 to 40 percent of their daily calories from fat.

Researchers at the University of Delaware found that for every calorie expended, children burn more body fat than adults do. Kids also use up more fat than do adults by virtue of the normal growth process like bone development. A low-fat diet may not meet the energy needs required for proper growth and development of young children. Do not offer your child a low-fat diet without the advice of your pediatrician.

All fats are not created equally, however. Here's a look at the role different fats play in your child's diet.

Healthy Fats

These fats are a healthy choice for growing bodies. Common sources for monounsaturated fats include:

- Liquid oils such as olive, canola, safflower, and grapeseed
- Avocados
- Safely chopped nuts

MONOUNSATURATED FATS

Monounsaturated fats are healthy fats that provide nutrients to help develop and maintain the body's cells. They're also rich in vitamin E, a powerful antioxidant, and have been proven to reduce "bad" cholesterol in the blood and reduce the risk of heart disease and stroke later in life.

POLYUNSATURATED FATS

Polyunsaturated fats have all of the benefits of monounsaturated fats while also providing essential fatty acids that your body needs but can't produce on its own. These essential fatty acids are known as omega-3 and omega-6 fatty acids and have a host of benefits, in the right proportions.

Omega-3 fatty acids play a key role in brain development, cardiovascular health, and immune system function. They're also important to the eyes, joints, and nervous system development. They are an essential part of everyone's diet and are especially crucial in the early years. Your baby's brain will grow to about three times its size in the first year of life and it needs adequate omega-3 fatty acids to ensure proper development. Infants up to 12 months should have 0.5 gram of omega-3 fatty acids a day. That's the amount in a 1-ounce (28 g) portion of salmon. Remember, your child is also getting omega-3 fatty acids through breast milk or enhanced formula.

A BABY'S DIET SHOULD CONSIST OF 10 TO 20 PERCENT MORE FAT THAN AN ADULT'S DIET IN ORDER TO SUPPORT HER RAPID GROWTH AND HER ABILITY TO METABOLIZE FATS AT A FASTER RATE.

Omega-3 fatty acids are strongly linked to behavior and learning in children. Unfortunately, the typical American diet is low in omega-3 fatty acids and high in omega-6 fatty acids. Too many omega-6s cause inflammation and disease, and we consume too many by eating packaged, processed foods. This imbalance can result in a wide range of physical and mental health disorders, including ADHD, dyslexia, dyspraxia, and other related behavioral and learning issues.

In a recent study, researchers at the University of Oxford found a direct correlation between the level of omega-3 DHA (an essential fatty acid) in a child's blood and his or her ability to concentrate and learn. The study looked at 493 children aged 7 to 9 who performed below average in reading comprehension. Researchers found that concentrations of DHA and other omega-3 fatty acids were well below the recommended levels. Parent reports of these children showed that 90 percent of the underperforming children were not eating the recommended two portions of fish a week and almost 10 percent of the children tested never ate any fish.

Your child will get omega-3 fatty acids through your breast milk or an enhanced formula. Once she starts to self-feed with solid foods, it's important to introduce some low-mercury fish options, such as anchovies, catfish, flounder, haddock, mackerel, salmon, and whitefish. Canned salmon is a healthy, easy option (bones have already been removed). However, you can feed your child any fish you are eating provided you carefully remove any bones and cut it into small pieces.

Omega-3 fatty acids can also be found in green leafy vegetables, soy, legumes, and flax seeds; however, the body does not convert vegetarian omega-3 fats into a usable form as readily as animal-based fats. Fish remains the best way to get the omega-3 fatty acids you need.

Although omega-6 fatty acids are important, they are abundant in most diets and you don't need to go out of your way to make sure your baby is getting enough. In fact, it's more common to eat more than enough omega-6 fatty acids, throwing off the delicate balance of omega-6 and omega-3 fatty acids.

Go Coconuts!

Coconut oil is a healthy way for your child to get her fill of saturated fats. Coconut oil is beneficial for parents and kids alike. Studies have found that coconut oil can improve digestive health and dental hygiene, help your body repair damaged DNA, and slow brain aging.

Ideally, you should have a ratio of 1:1 to 1:5 of omega-3 to omega-6 fatty acids. Because Western diets are often low in omega-3 fatty acids and high in omega-6, that ratio is closer to 1:16 in the average person. This excessive amount of omega-6 fatty acids throws the body into a constant inflammatory mode and can promote a host of illnesses ranging from cancer and cardiovascular disease to autoimmune diseases.

A recent study found that changing ratios to 1:2.5 reduced cell proliferation in patients with colorectal cancer, and lowering the ratio decreased the risk of breast cancer. Reducing to a ratio to 1:5 had profound effects on patients with asthma, whereas a ratio of 1:10 had the reverse effect.

Even though omega-6 fatty acids are healthy, you need not actively promote them in your child's diet. Sources rich in omega-6 fatty acids include vegetable oils such as sunflower, peanut, canola, and soy oils and fish and tofu. To help reduce omega-6s in your child's, and your family's, diet and to help balance the ratio of omega-3 and omega-6 fatty acids, use monounsaturated oils over vegetables oils in food preparation whenever possible, and limit processed foods.

SATURATED FATS

Saturated fats get a bad rap for raising cholesterol, but children don't need to avoid them entirely. Babies need saturated fats to support growth and development. Saturated fats also help calcium be effectively incorporated into your children's bones. Saturated fats occur naturally in foods that come from animal sources, including meat and dairy products. They may also exist in baked goods and fried foods and are in oils such as coconut, palm, and palm kernel. Choose wisely—we are not recommending offering fried foods to your child on a daily basis. Balance is the key.

TRANS FATS

Trans fats are the one fat type that should be avoided in your child's diet whenever possible. Trans fats have no health benefits and have an unhealthy effect on cholesterol levels, causing fatty deposits in the arteries. If your child starts eating trans fats at a young age it will contribute to this buildup over time and can increase her risk of a heart attack, stroke, or blood clot later in life.

Avoid Trans Fats

The following tips can help you avoid trans fats in your family's diet:

- Choose products with zero grams of trans fats. Products containing less than 0.5 grams of trans fat can round down to zero grams.
- Check for partially hydrogenated oil in the ingredients list, and avoid those products that contain it.
- Avoid fried foods entirely.
- Make your own baked goods, including pizza crusts, so that you can control the added fats.

Although some meat and dairy products contain small amounts of naturally occurring trans fats, you should aim to avoid the most abundant form of trans fats, which are artificially made. Trans fats come from foods that contain partially hydrogenated oil, which is formed when hydrogen is added to liquid oil, turning it into a solid fat. Manufacturers often use trans fats to extend the shelf life of packaged and processed foods. Some restaurants also use partially hydrogenated oil in their deep fryers because it doesn't have to be changed as often as other oils do. Trans fats are common in margarine, shortening, store-bought baked goods, snacks (such as chips, crackers, and microwave popcorn), frozen pizzas, premade pizza and cookie dough, ready-to-use frosting, and fried foods.

Fiber

While it was once believed that babies couldn't handle fiber, we now know that fiber is an essential part of digestive health. Insufficient fiber can lead to constipation and bowel issues.

Fiber is abundant in many healthy foods, so if you're feeding your baby well, chances are she's getting enough fiber. Balance is key, and you don't want to add too much fiber all at once. If your baby is having bowel or constipation issues you may want to look at the type of fiber you are feeding her.

There are two types of fiber: soluble and insoluble. Soluble fiber is abundant in lentils, beans, fresh fruits, and vegetables, and insoluble fiber is found primarily in whole grains and cereals. Insoluble fiber absorbs liquid and adds bulk to stools, but too much of a good thing can be problematic. Too much insoluble fiber is usually the issue when someone experiences gas pains or bloating as a result of excess fiber. Soluble fiber dissolves in water and forms a gel to help soften stool. It is less likely to be an issue with gas and pain.

Children should get about 14 grams of fiber for every 1,000 calories they eat. For a one-year-old that's about 19 grams of fiber a day. Baby rice cereal, refined white foods, and too much cheese and dairy have all been linked to constipation.

Vitamins

Vitamins perform a wide variety of functions in the body, such as assisting in the formation of red blood cells, helping release energy from food, supporting a healthy metabolism, and boosting the immune system. In the first year of life your child will get most of the vitamins he needs through breast milk or formula. At six months your child will gradually start to fulfill most of his vitamin requirements through food, and by a year he should be able to get all of the vitamins he needs by eating a balanced, healthy diet. There is no need to supplement except in a few instances.

VITAMIN D

Vitamin D is responsible for normal growth and development and the formation and maintenance of healthy bones and teeth. It also influences the absorption and metabolism of certain minerals and is necessary for proper muscle functioning and immunity.

Vitamin D is primarily produced in the skin after exposure to ultraviolet light; there are also small amounts in eggs, fortified milk, and fatty fish. Since your baby will not be receiving a lot of direct sunlight you need to supplement with vitamin D unless she is drinking enhanced formula, as there is not enough vitamin D in breast milk. Supplement with 400 international units (IU) of liquid vitamin D until around 12 months or until your baby is drinking whole cow's milk and eating oily fish and eggs on a regular basis.

VITAMIN B_{12}

Vitamin B_{12} plays a role in DNA synthesis and regulation, helps facilitate cell synthesis, and aids in the proper functioning of the nervous system, among other key roles. It is found in animal products and fish so is only a concern for strict vegetarians. You should talk to your doctor about possible supplementation if you or your baby is vegetarian. Although vitamin deficiencies are rare, talk to your doctor if you have any concerns or notice any growth delays, increased illnesses, bleeding gums, or rough skin.

Minerals

Even though minerals play many important roles in your child's health and development, they are only needed in very small amounts. In the first year, breast milk, formula, and the slow introduction of foods will meet your child's needs, with a few possible exceptions.

IRON

Your baby's iron stores will start to deplete themselves around six months of age. Iron plays a crucial role in the formation of red blood cells and transporting oxygen from the lungs to the rest of the body. A baby 7 to 12 months of age needs 11 milligrams of iron and a child 1 to 3 years of age needs 7 milligrams of iron a day.

Signs or Symptoms of Iron Deficiency

If you notice any of these symptoms in your baby, please ask your doctor about having your baby screened for iron deficiency.

- Fatigue
- Weakness
- Pale skin
- Slow cognitive and social development
- Increased susceptibility to infections
- Difficulty maintaining body temperature
- Inflammation of the tongue

Many parents turn to iron-enriched cereals, but the iron in these baby cereals is relatively low and it's poorly absorbed. A much better choice is to slowly start introducing iron-rich foods, such as meat, fish, beans, lentils, soy, oatmeal, green veggies, and egg yolks, to your baby. Eating vitamin C–rich foods such as kiwi, tomatoes, and broccoli will help increase iron absorption. Including these foods in your child's diet should ensure that he meets the necessary iron requirements.

Babies who are born prematurely or have a low birth weight are at an increased risk of iron deficiency because their reserves will not be as high. Babies who drink cow's milk before the age of one, or drink more than 24 ounces (710 ml) of cow's milk a day after the age of one, are also at an increased risk. Cow's milk isn't a suitable source of iron for babies, and iron is found only in small quantities in breast milk.

Kids need 500 mg of calcium every day. Dairy option (left): 1 cup (240 ml) of whole milk and 2 ounces (57 g) of cheese. Vegan option (right): 1 cup (256 g) kidney beans, ½ cup (34 g) kale, ¼ cup (31 g) tempeh, small sweet potato, ¼ cup (36 g) almonds, ¼ cup (38 g) figs, 1 cup (240 ml) fortified almond milk

CALCIUM

Calcium helps build strong bones and teeth. It also helps with heart rhythm, blood clotting, and muscle function. Calcium is stored in the bones, so if your child doesn't get enough from his diet his body will start to leech calcium from his bones, resulting in softening and weakening of the bones and osteoporosis later in life.

Your child will fulfill most of her calcium needs through breastfeeding or formula for the first year of life. After that, toddlers up to age 3 need 500 milligrams of calcium a day—the amount in 2 cups (470 ml) of milk or 1 cup (235 ml) of milk and 2 ounces (56 g) of cheese. If your child cannot eat dairy, you should talk to your doctor about possible calcium supplementation, as over 50 percent of calcium in U.S. diets comes from dairy products.

Summary of Early Nutritional Needs

- Limit simple carbohydrates, especially white sugar and flour.
- Feed your baby healthy protein choices, such as meat, fish, beans, lentils, eggs, and tofu.
- Focus on including brain-boosting omega-3 fatty acids in your child's diet. Your baby should ideally eat low-mercury fish at least twice a week.
- Avoid trans fats whenever possible.

- Fiber is important for your baby's digestive health.
- Supplement your child's diet for the first year with 400 IUs of vitamin D.
- If you or your baby is vegetarian, talk to your doctor about possible vitamin B_{12} deficiency.
- Include iron-rich foods such as beef, fish, and spinach starting at six months.

- CHAPTER 7 -

Self-Feeding Safety: Hazards, Allergies, and Special Diets

"With my first baby I was terrified of her choking," recalls Heather Donoghue, a Toronto-based mother of three. "I fed her purees until she was 13 months and now I'm paying the price." Donoghue's daughter, now eight, has always been a picky eater and Donoghue feels that the extended puree use may be partially to blame. "My oldest daughter has always been the worst eater of all my kids," she says. She still has a preference for creamy foods and Donoghue has to give her daughter smoothies to help her get her fill of fruits and vegetables.

By the time Donoghue had her second and third kids, she'd relaxed a bit about the choking worries, offering solid foods earlier. Her son, now two, ate his first solids at seven months and she's convinced that eating solid foods earlier has made a difference in his acceptance of foods.

Choking Concerns

The fear of choking is the number one reason parents delay the start of solid foods and avoid letting their infant self-feed. It's a natural concern as a first-time parent. We are a mere click away from scary statistics about children and choking—but let's get the facts straight.

Choking is the leading cause of injury among children, and babies and toddlers are at the greatest risk. Most children who choke to death do so on food rather than other objects. In fact, one American child dies every five days as a result of choking on food. More than 10,000 children are taken to the emergency room each year with food-choking injuries.

However, none of this means you need to live in fear of choking. We'll help you ensure that your child has a safe eating experience. You don't want your child to miss out on all the many benefits of early self-feeding due to fear. Instead, arm yourself with knowledge on how best to safely proceed.

We've already discussed the many benefits of self-feeding, starting at around six to eight months of age: fewer mealtime battles now and in the future, healthier eating behaviors, a reduced risk of obesity, greater convenience, shared family mealtimes, and developmental advantages. However, many parents remain reluctant to start self-feeding due to choking worries. Studies show that some health care professionals are also reluctant to recommend early self-feeding because of their concerns surrounding a potential increased risk of choking.

Know the Risks

Thirty percent of mothers who practice baby-led weaning reported at least one choking episode. The most common culprit is raw apple. While proper swallowing techniques can help reduce the risk, the most important thing is to never leave your child unattended while she's eating.

In most cases, worries about increased choking come from inexperience with proper self-feeding practices and a lack of knowledge of safe first foods and safe feeding practices. Here's what you need to know to keep your baby safe, while offering all of the benefits of early self-feeding.

RESPECT YOUR BABY'S TONGUE REFLEX

If you've ever tried to feed purees to a four-month-old you have likely noticed that the baby's first instinct is to use his tongue to push the food right back out. That's the baby's innate tongue reflex (first mentioned in chapter 3) telling you that he is too young to handle solid foods.

From birth until around four months of age, your baby's tongue will naturally push anything that enters the mouth outward. This is a tongue reflex that is designed to protect your baby from choking. Babies who still have this reflex are too young to handle swallowing anything other than liquids via breast or bottle (or alternative methods utilized in feeding therapy) and should not be given any solid food, including purees.

In fact, there is a direct correlation between early feeding practices and choking deaths. A British study looked at the number of choking deaths in infants and compared them to early feeding practices at the time. The study found that childhood deaths from choking were at a high in 1974, with 144 yearly deaths by choking in children up to 4 years. The numbers remained fairly consistent until they started to dramatically decline in 1980, reaching a low in the final year of the test (1984), with combined yearly choking deaths in England and Wales at 46.

The most significant reason for this decline was the dramatic decrease in choking deaths in children under the age of six months. In 1974 there were 104 deaths in babies 5 months and under. In 1984, there were just 24. Experts feel that the reason for this decline in infant choking deaths is that feeding practices changed, with increasing numbers of parents waiting until 6 months to introduce solid foods. In 1975, 85 percent of infants received solids prior to reaching 3 months of age and 45 percent received solids before 2 months. By 1980, the number of infants receiving solids before 3 months had dropped to 55 percent.

Despite the increased choking risk associated with introducing solid foods prior to six months of age, many parents still feel the need to feed their babies solid foods too early. In a 2013 study by the American Centers for Disease Control and Prevention, 40 percent of mothers surveyed said they gave their baby solid food before their child reached four months of age. Nine percent of parents in the survey started feeding their baby solids at just four weeks of age.

For more than 20 years the American Academy of Pediatrics has recommended parents feed their babies solid foods no earlier than 4 months of age. Recently their guidelines changed that timeline to six months. Developmentally, a child younger than six months is not ready to handle solid foods, even if you spoon-feed purees to her.

Respect your baby's tongue reflex. Prior to four months all babies will naturally push food out of their mouth. If you try to override your baby's tongue reflex you are increasing your child's choking risk.

Between four and six months the tongue reflex will begin to integrate, allowing the natural progression from exclusive breastfeeding or formula to the introduction of solid foods. This reflex serves another purpose: a baby learns from the reflex over time and gradually discovers how to *intentionally* push unwelcome food or objects forward, rather than backward. Wait to feed your child solid foods until this reflex has begun to integrate and only appears occasionally. When you introduce purees at this stage, your child will focus on how to move his tongue in such a way that it pushes purees to the back of the mouth.

IN A RECENT STUDY PUBLISHED IN THE *JOURNAL OF PEDIATRICS*, MORE THAN ONE-THIRD OF MOMS INTRODUCED SOLID FOODS PRIOR TO THEIR BABY REACHING FOUR MONTHS OF AGE. THE WIDELY ACCEPTED RECOMMENDATION IS SIX MONTHS.

KNOW THE DIFFERENCE BETWEEN CHOKING AND GAGGING

Before you start self-feeding, it's important to know that choking and gagging are two different experiences. Gagging is very common in all infants and can persist throughout infancy. Gagging is nature's way of protecting the airway, where true choking occurs. It is another internal defense mechanism to keep babies from swallowing things that they shouldn't eat or can't handle yet.

Gagging is an uncomfortable sensation. It happens when the soft palate suddenly elevates the jaw, thrusts forward and down, and the back of the tongue lifts up and forward. In between the gags, a child is still able to breathe, cry, and make vocal noises.

While some gagging is expected and protective, you want to avoid doing things that will cause excessive gagging. If your baby is gagging too much, chances are she is not ready for the food you are feeding her. Excessive gagging can give your infant an upsetting first experience with food and can even induce vomiting. Repeated gagging leads to repeated vomiting and irritation of the esophagus. Too many episodes and your child will associate eating, the feeding chair, and any mealtime experience with negative emotions and memories.

An infant under six months of age has a gag reflex that is triggered when the back three-quarters of the tongue is stimulated. As a result, gagging is common. Starting around six or seven months of age the tongue area that stimulates a gag reflex area starts to recede. Proponents of baby-led weaning argue that this is one of the advantages of starting finger foods at six months. The gag reflex has receded enough that most babies won't gag excessively, but the reflex is still very effective at keeping large pieces of food to the front of the mouth, only allowing well-masticated food to reach the back of the mouth for swallowing. Every child has a different sensory system and touch receptors that signal the gag reflex to activate. Your baby's gag reflex may be more sensitive than another baby's.

To help your baby learn to control the activation of the reflex, be sure to encourage him to mouth toys with a variety of textures. Choose toys with soft corners and chewies with long "arms" or "necks" that will reach farther back on the tongue. If that proves to be too stimulating, gradually work up to those types of toys by first offering wooden baby rings to fist and chew or toys with stubby appendages. Most of all, keep it positive and fun so that your baby continues to challenge himself and explore his toys more and more.

By about nine months of age, only the back third of the tongue will stimulate a gag reflex, so gagging while eating will be greatly reduced. Most children at this age can eat with minimal or no gagging. Eventually, the gag reflex will shift even more posteriorly as the child learns to tolerate the stimulation of eating.

Choking is very different from gagging and can be extremely dangerous. Choking happens when food or another substance obstructs the airway. While gagging can be loud and animated, choking has either no sound or intermittent, soft, odd sounds. For this reason you should never leave your baby unattended while eating. You will not be able to hear if she is choking and needs help.

WHY BABIES ARE PRONE TO CHOKING

Typically, a full-term infant is developmentally able to suck and swallow. She is also equipped with involuntary reflexes, including suckling (a forward-backward movement), the bite reflex that leads to learning to chew, gagging, coughing, and glottic closure to help protect against aspiration during swallowing. Yet in spite of all this, a young child's airway is more vulnerable to obstruction than that of an older child or adult in many ways.

1. **Babies have smaller throats.**
   The smaller diameter of a child's throat makes her more susceptible to blockage by small objects. In particular, the larynx—commonly thought of as the "voice box" and the narrowest part of the upper airway— is extremely small in children under the age of one. When choking occurs in children under 12 months of age, most inhaled foreign bodies are found in the larynx. In older children, more food or objects are found lodged in the trachea or bronchi.

   Because of this small opening, children under one year of age should have their food cut into smaller pieces—pea-size cubes—or be given large pieces of soft food to hold in their fist and mouth them so they will easily dissolve and break down.

Signs of Choking

- Gasping for breath
- Infant may wave arms or grab at throat
- Turns blue around the lips and beneath the eyes
- Staring with an open mouth while drooling
- Intermittent odd sounds

2. **A smaller airway means a decreased resistance to airflow.** Even small changes in the cross-section or diameter of the airway can lead to dramatic changes in airway resistance and the ability for adequate airflow. As the diameter of the airway increases, airflow increases by a power of four. The younger the child, the more reduced his airflow and the higher his risk of choking.

Because of this reduced airway resistance, young children are at an increased risk of choking if they are sick or suffering from excess mucus. Mucus and secretions will further reduce the radius of the airway, and may also form a seal around the piece of food that's being swallowed, making it more difficult to dislodge if it gets stuck. Common medical conditions such as reflux (often termed chronic spitting up or gastroesophageal reflux disease [GERD]) can cause inflammation and swelling in the laryngeal area, thus impacting the airway and increasing the risk of choking.

3. **Babies have a weaker cough.** The cough of a baby isn't as strong as that in an older child or adult. When a young child coughs it is less effective in dislodging a complete or partial airway obstruction, especially during infancy.

4. **Young babies are just learning to chew.** When solid foods are first being introduced, your baby is experiencing a new sensation that requires the coordination of chewing, swallowing, and breathing. This takes time to develop. Until your baby has mastered this process she will be at an increased risk of choking.

While some of these skills come with development and coordination, your baby's chewing technique will not be fully developed until he has a sufficient amount of teeth. Your child will start to get his front teeth around six months. After this your baby will be able to bite off a piece of food with his incisors. He will, however, be unable to grind certain foods adequately in preparation for swallowing.

The molars required for chewing and grinding food do not erupt until approximately one and a half years of age. Although choking risk is reduced at this time, mature mastication abilities take even longer to develop. Your child will still be at an increased choking risk until she has mastered the chewing and grinding technique by about age four. Children with developmental and neurologic impairment may take longer to master proper chewing techniques.

LEARNING TO SWALLOW FIRST

It's unknown whether children following baby-led weaning choke more than children who are spoon-fed purees. In a 2012 study in the *British Medical Journal*, 30 percent of parents who followed baby-led weaning reported one or more episodes of choking.

However, all of the parents who reported choking also reported that their infant independently dealt with the choking by expelling the food from her mouth through gagging and/or coughing. The parents did not have to intervene with any type of rescue or first aid.

Although we can't be sure the choking rate is higher with children who follow baby-led weaning, the gagging rate is definitely higher. You can reduce the risk of excessive gagging, and likelihood of choking, by teaching your baby to suck purees off a spoon as a bridge to learning to eat foods for self-feeding.

Purees have a purpose. They teach your baby to swallow comfortably. Use them for this purpose and then move on to solid foods. Experts agree that you can get the benefits of baby-led weaning while reducing the fear and increased risk of choking by teaching your baby to swallow with purees before introducing handheld and finger foods. Start with purees, then follow up with self-feeding a variety of tastes and textures, and you can get all the benefits of baby-led weaning while keeping choking risks to a minimum.

USE SAFE FIRST FOODS

When parents speak out about any choking experiences they've encountered, most of them are a result of improper food choices. In a 2011 study published in *Maternal Child Nutrition*, raw apple was to blame in over 60 percent of the choking instances in baby-led weaning.

Be careful—you may have been led to believe that you can feed your baby anything you eat. This is not true. A six-month-old has few if any teeth and is just learning the chewing process. A baby is likely not able to chew hard or tough foods yet. It's a parent's job to provide safe food choices that a new eater can handle. This is yet another advantage of beginning with purees, moving on to soft solids, and gradually working up to chewable foods.

Babies should not be given anything too hard. They don't have the teeth or chewing skills to break it down safely. For example, apples pose a high choking risk. It is easy for a large chunk to snap off, for the baby to swallow it, and for it to become lodged in her throat. Until your baby has developed chewing skills and enough molars to grind up hard foods, anything hard should be avoided and anything tough should be cut into small pea-size pieces that are safe if baby accidently swallows them without chewing first. Once your baby has developed grasping skills for thin slices or strips, consider cutting raw apples into matchsticks and letting your child nibble on those to experience the crunch. Advanced grasping skills necessary for holding more fragile foods emerge around 15 months of age. In the meantime, soften apples and other crunchy foods by steaming them first.

The ideal width to cut veggie or fruit sticks is about the width of your pinky finger. Steam them until they are soft enough that no hard, small pieces will break off, but not so soft that they crumble and fall apart in your baby's hand as he is trying to eat them. Blanching is another option for older kids who have molars emerging at around 12 months. The ice water bath will stop the cooking just in time to leave a bit of crunch. Also, more water will be absorbed during the blanching process and the food will be softer, moister, and easier to chew with new molars while still offering the crunch and flavor that kids will love. Steaming vegetables rather than boiling them in water allows the vegetables to retain more nutrients and keeps them tender without getting waterlogged and mushy.

How to Steam Fruit or Vegetables

1 Place a steamer basket in a pot and fill with water just to reach the bottom of the basket. Place the veggies in the basket. (Cutting them into smaller pieces will reduce cooking time.) Place a lid on the pot and bring the water to a boil over medium-high heat.

2 Steam the vegetables until soft but not mushy, checking tenderness with a paring knife or fork.

There are soft fruits that are suitable to give to your baby raw and cut into sticks, such as avocado, pears, and banana, as long as they are ripe. Still other fruits lie in that in between phase. Fruits like plums, cantaloupe, and peaches are soft enough that they don't have to be steamed, but still hard enough that they could pose a choking risk if a large piece comes off. Cut these items into small, pea-size cubes. Cubes are easier for your child to

Safe Finger Foods for Early and Emergent Eaters (6-12 Months)

Soft, ripe fruits (cut into strips or appropriate safe-size chunks)

Avocado

Bananas

Grapes

Melons

Pears

Plums

Strawberries

Tomatoes

Soft-roasted fruits and vegetables (cooled and cut into strips or safe-size chunks)

Apples

Asparagus

Bananas

Bell peppers

Beets

Broccoli

Carrots

Kale

Lentils

Mushrooms

Parsnips

Pears

Peas

Plums

Potatoes

Spinach and naturally soft greens

String beans

Sweet Potatoes

Tomatoes

Yams

Zucchini

Grains (add an oily dressing or a bit of melted cheese for easier handling and swallowing)

Barley

Brown or white rice (in limited quantities; see page 75)

Buckwheat

Cous cous

Crackers: meltable and healthy options

Oatmeal

Muffins and soft breads (cut into strips or safe-size chunks)

Quinoa

Toast with an oily spread, such as avocado

Proteins (cooked, cooled, and cut into strips or safe-size chunks)

"Smushed" soft beans

Cooked eggs

Fish (remove all bones)

Meats (soft): brisket, tenderloin, meatballs

Tofu

Dairy

Soft cheeses thinly spread on foods listed above

Harder cheeses in pea-sized cubes

feel in his mouth, less frustrating than round items for your child to pick up, and won't roll off the tray.

Meat is another potential choking hazard. Meat needs to be cut into small pea-size cubes and should not be overly hard or chewy. Although white chicken breast is a healthy food choice for adults, it's not the best first meat for your child because it is fibrous and can be difficult for young babies to chew. Dark meat chicken is moister and easier for children to chew. Be sure to avoid any marbled meat. Fat is tough to chew and poses a choking hazard. Instead, look toward softer beef and pork tenderloins, stewed beefs, or darker chicken and turkey meat. Ground beef is also a healthy choice.

How to Blanch Fruit or Vegetables

1 Cut up vegetables or hard fruit into small, bite-size pieces.

2 Prepare an ice bath with about twice as much water as ice.

3 Boil enough water to cover the veggies or fruit by at least 1 inch (2.5 cm). When the water is boiling, plunge the vegetables or fruit into the water for 1 to 2 minutes, then transfer to the ice bath.

HIGH-RISK FOODS

Foods associated with choking are usually hard, round and smooth, or pliable and not easily broken down. Hard or round and smooth items can slip easily into your child's airway, obstructing it either partially or completely. Pliable, unbending foods can be especially dangerous because they are difficult to expel.

It's easy to see why hot dogs are among the most dangerous foods in terms of choking hazard. A hot dog is cylindrical and a similar size to your child's airway. It's compressible, which allows it to wedge tightly into a child's hypopharynx and completely block the airway. Because of a hot dog's smooth texture, it is extremely difficult to expel. In fact, hot dogs account for 17 percent of all food-related asphyxiations among children younger than 10 years of age and two-thirds of all deaths from choking on meat products for children under the age of three. The problem is, hot dogs are a popular family food at home, in restaurants, and in the community. You'll need to be vigilant to ensure that your young child only eats hot dogs that are cut up appropriately.

Other high-risk foods include hard candy (especially flat lollipops such as those given out at many doctor's offices), peanuts and nuts, peanut butter, seeds, whole grapes, raw carrots, apples, popcorn, marshmallows, chewing gum, and sausages. Many of these foods are round (or can be bitten off into round pieces), creating effective plugs for a small airway.

Although peanut butter may not seem like a choking hazard, its consistency can conform to your child's airway and form a tenacious seal that is difficult to dislodge or extract. This is similar to the effect of a latex balloon.

CHOKING IS MORE LIKELY WHEN CHILDREN ARE GIVEN HARD FOODS, SUCH AS RAW APPLE, OR ROUND COIN-SHAPED FOODS, SUCH AS SLICES OF HOT DOG.

Peanuts need to be chewed in a grinding motion, which is not well developed until at least four years of age. If offering nut butters or nuts to older children, make sure that it's as a thin layer on top of another food or cut up into pea-size pieces and given one at a time to any child that does not have molars and advanced chewing skills for grinding.

While certain natural foods like hard produce and peanuts rank high on the list of foods that cause choking hazards, it's interesting to note that many high-risk foods associated with choking are man-made. The characteristics of these engineered foods—such as hot dogs, hard candy, and marshmallows—are firm shapes that form a suction when they get stuck in the throat, making them more difficult to dislodge than natural food items.

Self-Feeding Safety

- Wait until your baby is six months of age before introducing solid foods.

- Read your baby's cues and don't introduce solid foods before she is developmentally ready.

- Respect your baby's tongue reflex that pushes food out of the mouth at first. It's designed to protect your baby from choking. Babies who consistently demonstrate this reflex are too young to handle swallowing anything other than liquids and should not be given any solid food, including purees.

- Choking and gagging are two different things. Gagging is nature's way of protecting the airway, where true choking occurs.

- While some gagging during the initial stages of self-feeding can be expected, excessive gagging can give your infant an unpleasant first experience with food.

- Choking happens when food or another substance obstructs the airway. While gagging can be loud and animated, choking has either no sound or intermittent, soft, odd sounds.

- Always seat your baby with proper positioning in a high chair with optimal stability.

- Children under one year of age should have their food cut into smaller pieces—pea-size cubes—or be given larger pieces of soft food that will easily dissolve and break down in their mouth.

- Avoid high-risk foods such as hard foods, like raw apple, or round coin-shaped foods, such as slices of hot dog.

- Never leave your baby unattended while eating.

- Take an infant CPR course and be prepared in case choking does occur.

REDUCE THE RISK OF CHOKING

In addition to avoiding high-risk choking foods, there are a few simple steps parents can do to limit choking risks.

- It is essential that your child sit upright at mealtime. Your child should be seated safely in a high chair, be well supported, and be able to sit tall and keep her head up.
- Your child should no longer have the tongue reflex when he starts to eat. Teach your child to swallow first with purees and then move on to finger foods.
- An adult must be present and watching when your child is eating.
- Take an infant CPR course and know how to come to your child's aid if she does choke on something.
- While you want mealtime to be a fun family time, distraction during eating by laughing or rowdy playing increases the risk of inhalation and choking. Engage in light banter but have your child refrain from eating if he is giggling or fooling around. Technology is extremely distracting and is best kept away from the table for social and safety reasons.
- When your child gets older and starts to walk around, encourage her to sit at the table and focus on her food rather than grazing as she cruises about. Running around during mealtime will increase the risk of choking at any age.

Dealing with Food Allergies

It was only a few decades ago that having a kid with allergies in a classroom was an irregularity rather than the norm. Growing up, Nancy suffered from dairy allergies and her younger brother Michael was allergic to both dairy and wheat. They were isolated cases at their school. Back then, most parents weren't typically aware of allergies, and no one ever made different "allergen-free" food at parties. Nancy remembers bringing her own food or going without. Even back then, kids' parties consisted primarily of pizza, chocolate cake, and ice cream—all big no's for anyone with a dairy allergy.

How a few decades changes things. Allergy rates have tripled in the past 10 to 15 years in North America, Britain, and Australia. It's now estimated that roughly 15 million Americans have food allergies, and that allergies affect 1 in every 13 children—that's roughly two kids in every classroom. The rate of increase is alarming! Experts aren't certain as to why the increase in allergies has been so dramatic in the past few decades. However, there are a few theories.

SANITIZER DEPENDENCE

We live in a society that is obsessed with hygiene. Many parents carry alcohol-based hand sanitizers and use them on a daily basis. There are also wall-mounted hand sanitizer machines everywhere from doctors' offices and museums to daycares and indoor play areas.

While proper hand washing is a vital part of warding off colds and flus, it's believed that kids may need to be exposed to some germs in order to train their immune systems to know the difference between harmful and harmless irritants.

Researchers have found that kids growing up on farms have lower rates of asthma and other allergies. It's possible that the large amounts of bacteria and other microbes present on farms may play a protective role against developing allergies. Specifically, researchers believe that farm animals increase exposure to germ components called endotoxins. These endotoxins stimulate the body's immune response, decreasing allergic inflammation.

EVERY THREE MINUTES A FOOD ALLERGY REACTION SENDS SOMEONE TO THE EMERGENCY ROOM.

OVERUSE OF ANTIBIOTICS AND ACETAMINOPHEN

Some experts believe that excessive use of drugs such as antibiotics and acetaminophen is at least partially responsible for the increase in allergies. Recently, researchers at the University of Minnesota found a link between antibiotic use in infancy and allergies. Antibiotic use early in life may eradicate key gut bacteria that can help immune cells mature. These cells play an essential role in keeping the immune system functioning when confronted with allergens. Even if the gut gets the helpful bacteria back later in life, the immune system will remain impaired.

An infant's gastrointestinal tract is an ever-changing system. In fact, an infant's age can be predicted within 1.3 months based on the maturity of his gut bacteria. Because an infant's gut bacteria are quickly changing and delicate in early life, alterations caused by antibiotics can have more severe health implications than they would in an adult.

Use extreme caution when giving antibiotics to young children. While there are cases when antibiotics are necessary, they are often overprescribed. Each year 75 million antibiotics are prescribed to children in the United States—roughly one for every child. Antibiotics account for one-fourth of all medications given to children, and experts estimate that this number is up to 50 percent higher than necessary.

Other studies show that the increased use of acetaminophen in children might have an impact on the rising asthma and allergy rates. In a study published in *the Iranian Journal of Allergy, Asthma, and Immunology*, the prevalence of asthma-type allergies was 11.3 percent greater in children who took acetaminophen in the first year of life. Children who had taken acetaminophen in the past 12 months were also at an increased risk of eczema, a common precursor to allergies.

While we're not suggesting avoiding medications completely—there are instances where drugs play an essential role in your child's well-being—do use caution. Assess the pros and cons with a doctor and ensure the any medications taken—especially in the early years of life—are necessary.

VITAMIN D DEFICIENCY

Some experts believe that a lack of vitamin D could be partially to blame for rising rates of allergies, particularly asthma. Vitamin D is essential for lung and immune system development. Without adequate amounts, the immune system may be more vulnerable to allergies.

THE AVERAGE PERSON RECEIVES AT LEAST 80 PERCENT OF THEIR VITAMIN D THROUGH UV-INDUCED SKIN PRODUCTION. VITAMIN D CANNOT BE PRODUCED IF YOU ARE WEARING SUNSCREEN.

Children tend to spend more time indoors than in past generations. In fact, most American adults and children spend just 10 percent of available daylight hours outside. When children are outdoors they are often in the shade or covered in sunscreen, especially in the early years of life. This decreased exposure to sunlight results in reduced vitamin D production.

Supplementing with 400 IUs of vitamin D each day is an effective way to help combat vitamin D deficiencies. Short-duration exposure to the sun is a good thing. Aim to give children over the age of 6 months 10 to 15 minutes of exposure to sunlight (without sunscreen) on as many days as possible. Avoid midday sun when rays are strongest.

WHEN TO TRY HIGH-RISK FOODS

There is another theory as to why the rate of food allergies is on the rise, and it's a little more controversial. There has been a tendency in the past few decades to hold off on introducing high-allergy-risk foods. Could this early avoidance of high-risk foods be partially to blame for the increase in allergy rates?

There has been a flip-flop in the past few decades as to when to first introduce high-risk foods. In 2000, experts advised that dairy shouldn't be introduced to any children until age one, eggs until age two, and peanuts until age three. Some experts also advised that pregnant women avoid eating high-risk foods such as nuts. "These recommendations weren't really based on anything but fear," says Dr. Scott Sicherer, professor of pediatrics, researcher at the Jaffe Food Allergy Institute at Mount Sinai in New York, and author of *Food Allergies: A Complete Guide to Eating When Your Life Depends on It.* There wasn't a single study proving that there was any benefit to holding off on the introduction of high-risk foods in otherwise healthy children.

The thinking behind these avoidance tactics was that allergic reactions could be potentially life threatening; thus, it was assumed best to avoid the foods early on to avoid the risk. This reasoning is like avoiding getting in a car because you might get in an accident. Sure, there is a chance you could have an accident. However, the benefits of getting where you need to go typically outweigh the perceived risk.

It's now been widely accepted that there is no benefit in holding off on the introduction of high-allergy-risk foods in healthy babies. Ironically, holding off on the introduction of nuts may actually put your child at an increased risk of developing allergies. In 2008, the American Academy of Allergy, Asthma and Immunology (AAAAI) rescinded its recommendation to hold off on the introduction of high-allergy-risk foods, provided that your child wasn't at a high risk of becoming allergic. As of 2008, the advice has been if you have a healthy, happy baby and no family history of allergies, you may introduce high-risk foods as soon as you introduce solids, provided they are not a choking hazard. However, even many doctors have been slow to adapt to the changes, and some continue to advise holding off on the introduction of some foods. "There is no reason to avoid specific allergens," says Sicherer. "It's ill-advised."

A child may be at risk of allergies if he experiences skin rashes such as eczema, has chronic vomiting, or has had a past allergic reaction to another food. "If you gave your eight-month-old milk and he broke out in hives, experts wouldn't have advised rushing to give him peanut butter," says Sicherer. However, a new study has changed that advice.

In June 2015, the AAAAI issued a statement on the importance of the early introduction of peanuts in all children, regardless of their allergy risk. This advice is based on a 2015 Learning Early About Peanut (LEAP) study published in

The Big Eight

Eight foods account for 90 percent of all allergic food reactions. These are:

- Dairy
- Soy
- Eggs
- Wheat
- Peanuts
- Fish
- Tree nuts
- Shellfish

The New England Journal of Medicine that provided new evidence to support early, rather than delayed, peanut introduction for children who are at a high risk of contracting allergies. The study was developed because researchers noticed a striking difference between peanut allergy rates in Jewish children living in the United Kingdom versus those living in Israel. Both children had similar ancestry, but the U.K.-based children were 10 times as likely to have an anaphylactic peanut allergy. The primary difference between the two groups of kids appeared to be the age of introduction of peanuts. While most children in the United Kingdom avoided peanuts in the first year of life, infants in Israel typically started eating peanut-based foods at around seven months of age. This started the hypothesis that the early introduction of peanuts may offer protection from the development of peanut allergies.

The LEAP study took place from 2006 to 2009 with a group of 640 infants between the ages of 4 and 11 months who had severe eczema, egg allergies, or both. Infants were randomly assigned to receive either no peanuts for the first two years of life or to receive an average of 7.7 grams of peanut protein each week for the first two years of feeding—that's the equivalent of six teaspoons of peanuts or 24 peanuts.

When the children were tested at 5 years of age, researchers found that introducing peanuts to high-allergy-risk kids between the ages of 4 and 11 months actually decreased their risk of developing peanut allergies by up to 80 percent. Early exposure appears to boost immune tolerance. Researchers still need to look at whether the high rates of peanut consumption needs to continue for life in order to receive the immunity benefits, or whether exposure in the early years is enough to help potentially ward off allergies.

While early introduction—in the first few months of solid foods—of peanut-based foods is recommended for every child, if your child has had eczema or other food allergies, or is otherwise high risk, you should talk to your pediatrician and/or an allergy specialist before introducing peanuts to ensure that your child is safely monitored.

CHILDREN CAN OUTGROW AN ALLERGY

In Nancy's case she was fortunate and outgrew her dairy allergies once she hit puberty. The same is true for many children with allergies to dairy, egg, and soy. These allergies typically begin in childhood and can dissipate by the age of 16, and often sooner. However, a recent study at Johns Hopkins University School of Medicine found that children can take longer to outgrow cow's milk and egg allergies. On the other hand, peanut, tree nut, fish, and shellfish allergies tend to be for life.

Ensuring Your Baby Gets Enough Food

Children tend to be capable of determining the amount of food they need, provided that a variety of healthy foods are presented to them on a continual basis. Your child's hunger and desire for different foods will vary from meal to meal and day to day, so don't become overly concerned with monitoring every single bite that goes into his mouth. You don't need to be worried if your child doesn't eat well at a particular meal.

Food Allergy Facts

- Food allergy rates have tripled in the past 10 to 15 years.

- One in every 13 children suffers from food allergies.

- Let your kid get dirty sometimes. Children may need to be exposed to some germs in order to train their immune systems to know the difference between harmful and harmless irritants.

- An infant's gut is extremely fast changing, and young bacteria are more sensitive to change, caused by things like antibiotics, than an adult's gastrointestinal tract is.

- Limit the use of antibiotics and acetaminophen, especially in the first few years of life.

- Supplement your child's diet with 400 IUs of vitamin D and make sure he gets some sunscreen-free exposure to the sun.

- Children who have skin rashes such as eczema, chronic vomiting, or a past allergic reactions are at an increased risk for food allergies.

- Introducing peanuts to high-allergy-risk kids between the ages of 4 and 11 months can decrease their risk of developing peanut allergies.

- Although early introduction of high-allergy-risk foods is encouraged at a young age, you should talk to a doctor if your child is high risk to ensure you do it safely.

- Your child is more likely to outgrow certain food allergies, such as dairy, eggs, and soy, than others.

- You can introduce all foods to your child, provided they are not a choking hazard, once she is old enough to start eating solid foods.

Rather than focus on what he's eating at each meal, or even each day, focus on what your child is eating over the course of a week. Maybe all he wants to eat one day is toast, but over the course of the week notice whether your child is getting a variety of healthy foods. Aside from some children with medical conditions and/or selective eating, most children are capable of monitoring their feeling of fullness if parents allow them to.

LOOK FOR STEADY, CONTINUOUS GROWTH

A steady growth pattern in height, weight, and head circumference is the best way to monitor whether your child is getting a sufficient amount of food. Your child's doctor should be plotting your child's growth on a chart. These growth charts represent the average for a normal child at a particular age. If your child's weight is at the 25th percentile, for example, it means that out of 100 normal children of the same age and sex, your child weighs more than 25 and less than 75.

Just like adults, children come in different sizes. In most cases you don't need to be concerned if your child is in the 10th percentile for height and weight—it just means she's a smaller kid. Rather than compare your children against others, growth charts are meant to monitor steady, continuous growth. Growing up, Melanie was always in the 99th percentile for height and 50th percentile for weight. That was normal for her, because her parents were both tall and of average weight. Nancy was also tall, and her boys both ranged in the 50th to 75th percentile for height and much lower for weight. Her eldest son stayed just below the 10th percentile for the first two years of life, and his personal growth was consistent. Her daughter was born prematurely, so she has always been around the 25th percentile for both height and weight—again, her growth has been consistent, so there have been no worries.

There will always be people in the 5th percentile and others in the 95th percentile. Most are somewhere in the middle. That's what makes it a bell curve! If your child is born in the 10th percentile for both height and weight and continues to hover around this percentile for the next year or two, your child is growing at a steady rate. If, however, your child is born in the 60th percentile, and at 6 months drops to the 40th and then at 8 months is down to the 30th, there may be an issue with the food intake your child is getting. Likewise, if your child is at the 30th percentile at 6 months and by 9 months she's at the 80th, you may be feeding your child too much.

Head circumference is closely monitored because it can affect a child's brain growth and cognitive development. Your pediatrician will alert you if she sees a stall in growth in this area.

The most important thing to remember is that growth charts are meant to monitor growth progress, not to compare your child against other children. As long as your child is on a steady upward trajectory, chances are he's getting enough food and is growing properly.

And of course, not all changes in percentiles are a signal of a problem. There are reasons for changes in growth trajectory. Your child may have had a growth spurt in height or started moving more, causing him to become thinner. Your doctor will be able to help you determine whether there is an issue with any change on his growth chart or if it is just a natural part of development.

Ask Whether Your Child Appears Healthy

If your child appears healthy, she probably is. Look at your child's energy level and temperament. Is she happy and eager to try new things? Have there been any recent changes in the way your child acts? Also, look at your child's eyes, skin, hair, nails, and teeth. If her eyes are dull, or her skin or hair is dry or cracked, it could be a sign of a nutritional deficiency and you should talk to your doctor.

DIAPER CHECK

Although you don't want to get too obsessive about bowel movements, it's a good idea to monitor your child's diaper from time to time, especially if you're concerned about his nutritional intake. Healthy children should have a solid stool once or twice a day and it should typically be brown in color. If your child's stools are sometimes orange, yellow, or green, don't panic. What your child eats can affect the color of his stools, especially in the early months of self-feeding. However, if your child's stools are consistently a light hue in color or your child is going for several days without having a bowel movement, you should consult your doctor.

CONSTIPATION IMPACTS APPETITE

Episodes of constipation lead to more constipation. As the stool hardens and bulks up in the intestine, the intestine begins to stretch to accommodate the size of the stool. Although the child may eventually have a bowel movement, the intestine remains stretched out in that particular spot, creating the perfect holding place for another large stool. Keeping stools a soft, solid consistency and having regular bowel movements will prevent constipation.

Talk with your child's doctor if your child is not having regular, comfortable bowel movements. When kids are constipated (especially babies and young children) it impacts appetite. Children will struggle to monitor their feelings of hunger and fullness on their own when they are constipated.

Monitor Health and Steady Growth

- Your child's hunger and desire for different foods will vary.

- Focus on what your child eats over the course of a week, rather than at each meal.

- A steady growth pattern is the best way to monitor whether your child is getting a sufficient amount of food.

- Ask yourself whether your child seems happy, has an appropriate energy level, and looks healthy.

- Healthy children should have a soft, solid stool once or twice a day and it should typically be brown in color.

Special Considerations for Vegetarian and Vegan Diets

The decision to be vegetarian or vegan—or to raise a vegetarian or vegan child—is highly personal. There are many factors that may come into play, such as animal rights and perceived health benefits. While it's possible to raise a healthy child with or without meat or dairy, there are some things parents considering vegetarianism or veganism should take into consideration.

WEIGHING THE POTENTIAL BENEFITS OF VEGETARIANISM

While many people choose to be vegetarian for ethical reasons, there is an increasing list of potential health benefits that experts say come from avoiding or eating less meat. These benefits include a reduced risk of heart attack and stroke, a lowered chance of diabetes, and an increase in overall longevity.

In a 2013 study out of the University of Oxford, 45,000 people, of whom 34 percent followed a vegetarian lifestyle, were analyzed. Researchers found the risk of heart disease was 32 percent lower in the vegetarians, even when factors such as age, smoking, alcohol intake, physical activity, educational level, and socioeconomic background were taken into account. Vegetarians had lower blood pressure and cholesterol levels than nonvegetarians, which is thought to be the main reason behind their reduced risk of heart disease. They also typically had lower body mass indices (BMI) and fewer cases of diabetes. Another study published in *Diabetes Care* found that vegetarians experience a 36 percent lower prevalence of metabolic syndrome than nonvegetarians. Metabolic syndrome is often a precursor to heart disease, diabetes, and stroke.

VEGETARIANISM MAY DELAY THE ONSET OF PUBERTY

The age of onset of puberty in girls has fallen dramatically in the past few decades. A recent study in *Pediatrics* found that 18.3 percent of Caucasian girls, 30.9 percent of Hispanic girls, and 42.9 percent of black girls had breast development by 8 years of age. These numbers are startling considering that earlier maturation in girls is associated with lower self-esteem, a less favorable body image, and an earlier onset of sexual intercourse. Early puberty also puts girls at an increased risk of endometrial and breast cancers. A study published in the *British Journal of Cancer* found that the risk of breast cancer was decreased by 4 to 9 percent for each year that menarche (or first menstrual period) was delayed.

Experts have found many potential causes for the earlier onset of puberty, including phthalates in plastics, and pesticides and hormones in meat and dairy. Eating hormone-laced meat may be especially significant in upsetting your child's delicate hormonal balance. A study by the Johns Hopkins University School of Hygiene and Public Health found that girls who consumed more animal protein and less vegetable protein between the ages of three and five had earlier menarche.

> ACCORDING TO A 2014 NATIONAL SURVEY CONDUCTED ON BEHALF OF THE VEGETARIAN RESOURCE GROUP, THERE ARE OVER TWO MILLION YOUTH VEGETARIANS AND HALF A MILLION YOUTH VEGANS IN THE UNITED STATES.

Although it may not be necessary to swear off meat completely, it does appear that there are benefits to decreasing the hormones ingested from meat and dairy either by choosing organic meats and dairy or by eating less of these foods when possible.

MEETING YOUR CHILD'S NUTRITIONAL NEEDS WITH A VEGETARIAN OR VEGAN DIET

Although the benefits of vegetarianism are well documented in many studies, you should still take special care to ensure that you are meeting all of your child's nutritional needs. You may decide that the perceived health benefits of following a vegetarian lifestyle aren't worth the risk of iron deficiency in your child, for example.

Does Vegetarianism Stunt Growth?

Some studies suggest that the growth of vegetarian children is more gradual than that of nonvegetarians. One study published in *Pediatrics* found that the average height and weight were slightly less for children following a vegetarian diet than for children eating meat. The largest height difference was observed at one to three years of age. However, most of this height gap had closed by the time the children reached 10 years of age, and final height and weight for vegetarian children were found to be comparable to those of meat-eating children. So while it appears that vegetarian children may grow a bit more slowly at first, they catch up later on. It's interesting to note that the same pattern is true for breastfed babies—they tend to grow more slowly than bottle-fed babies but catch up later on.

The American Dietetic Association has stated that well-planned vegetarian diets are healthful and nutritious for all stages of the life cycle, including pregnancy, lactation, infancy, and childhood. The key is that the diet needs to be well planned. When it comes to nutrients, plant foods are typically the preferred source because they are packed with health-promoting nutrients such as vitamins, minerals, phytochemicals, and fiber, while providing sufficient energy and protein in many cases.

Here are a few areas where a vegetarian or vegan diet could fall short and the precautions parents can take to ensure that their children are getting all the nutrients they need.

Iron: The iron in meat is often more readily absorbed than that from vegetarian sources. If you are raising a vegetarian or vegan child, make sure she gets plenty of iron-rich foods, such as dark leafy vegetables, beans, lentils, tofu, enriched whole grains, peas, nuts, and seeds. Also, vitamin C increases iron absorption. Feeding your child iron along with foods that are rich in vitamin C is an effective way to make sure your child is meeting her iron needs. Broccoli is a great choice as it's high in both iron and vitamin C.

Vitamin B12: Parents need to make sure their child's diet includes a regular source of vitamin B12, which is needed for healthy blood and nerve function. Eggs and dairy are rich in B12, so vegans will need to pay extra attention to incorporate it into their diet. Vitamin B12 is plentiful in many commercial cereals, fortified soy and rice milks, and nutritional yeast. You can check food labels for the words *vitamin B12* or *cyanocobalamin*. If you are concerned that your child is not getting sufficient foods with vitamin B12, talk to your doctor about a supplement.

Calcium: Calcium is a mineral responsible for building strong bones and teeth. Children who eat calcium-rich foods build up stores of calcium in their bones that will help them have strong bones for life. It's essential that you maximize your child's calcium intake early in life so that he can reach his peak bone mass. The ability to store calcium for bone growth ends in the late teen years, after which you can only maintain what is already stored in your bones.

While your child will continue to get calcium through breast milk in the first year of life, you should gradually start to introduce calcium-rich foods at six months. After the first year, many children will reach their calcium needs by eating dairy. A one-year-old should get 700 milligrams of calcium a day. A cup (235 ml) of whole milk has 276 milligrams of calcium and an ounce (28 g) of cheddar cheese has 204 milligrams of calcium, so children who eat two or three servings of dairy each day should have no problem meeting their calcium needs.

Foods High in Vitamin C

Asparagus	Mango
Avocado	Oranges
Berries	Papaya
Broccoli	Peppers
Brussels sprouts	Pineapple
Cabbage	Potatoes
Cauliflower	Rapini
Grapefruit	Snow peas
Guava	Strawberries
Kale	Sweet potatoes
Kiwi	Tomatoes

For vegans or children with dairy allergies, this minimum calcium requirement can be harder to fill. Foods such as beans, almonds, dried figs, sweet potatoes, collards, kale, broccoli, and Swiss chard all have calcium in smaller amounts. A whole cup (150 g) of sweet potatoes has just 40 milligrams of calcium, a cup (265 g) of kidney beans 62 milligrams of calcium, and a cup (70 g) of chopped kale has 101 milligrams of calcium. If your child can't eat dairy, look into calcium-fortified soy or almond milk and juices and talk to your doctor about a possible supplement.

Protein: Even if your child doesn't eat meat, it's not hard to fill his protein needs if he's eating a healthy diet. Kids don't need as much protein as you may think, and their needs can easily be met by eating beans, tofu, nuts, nut butters, dairy, and eggs.

REDUCING SALT INTAKE WILL HELP THE BODY RETAIN MORE CALCIUM.

Fat: Vegetarian, and especially vegan, diets tend to be low in fat. While this may be healthy for most adults, children—and especially babies—need more fat in their diets. If your child doesn't eat meat, fish, or dairy, make sure that she gets plenty of healthy fats through avocados, nuts and nut butters, seeds and seed butters, and full-fat soy. Omega-3 fatty acids are especially important for brain development at this age, so add foods such as flaxseed and flaxseed oil, chia and hemp seeds, Brussels sprouts, and cauliflower to boost your child's omega-3 count.

Some saturated fats are also important in the early years, so cooking with coconut oil is a healthy way to get a preferred source of saturated fats into your child's diet.

The main takeaway is that vegetarian and vegan diets can work for young children, provided that parents take special care in planning their meals. If you are omitting meat, fish, eggs, and/or dairy from your child's diet, then you need to make sure you are replacing these foods with healthy whole food choices, including more fruits and vegetables, beans, lentils, and nuts, and not simply adding more processed foods.

Facts about Vegetarian and Vegan Diets

- Studies have found a long list of benefits from following a vegetarian diet, including a reduced risk of heart attack, stroke, and diabetes; a delayed onset of puberty; and an increase in overall longevity.

- Include iron-rich foods, such as dark leafy vegetables, beans, lentils, tofu, enriched whole grains, peas, nuts, and seeds, in your child's diet. Eating vitamin C with iron-rich foods will increase iron absorption.

- Your child may need to supplement with vitamin B_{12} and calcium if she doesn't eat dairy.

- Make sure your child has a sufficient amount of healthy fats in his diet.

- CHAPTER 8 -
Table Manners, Messy Eating Solutions, and Tips for Dining Out

Developing a strong bond and a trusting relationship with their child is a priority for parents. Research shows that family mealtime plays a large role in building and nurturing that healthy relationship. It's proven that families who have frequent dinners together have closer relationships than families who do not dine together regularly.

Columbia University is performing an ongoing study looking at how parents can become more engaged in their children's lives. The researchers have found a direct relationship between parental engagement with their teenagers and drug and alcohol abuse. Researchers believe that by showing parents ways to strengthen the bond with their children they can decrease teenage drug and alcohol abuse.

Year after year the Columbia University surveys have consistently found that parents who eat dinner as a family on a regular basis have a closer relationship with their children. The 2012 study found that teenagers who have frequent family dinners (five or more times a week) are one and a half times more likely to say their parents know a lot about what's going on in their lives. On the other hand, 40 percent of teens in the study who ate dinner with their family fewer than three times a week reported that their parents knew very little or nothing at all about what was going on in their lives.

Eating dinner as a family also boosts the quality of relationships between parents and their children. Forty-nine percent of teens who enjoyed regular family mealtimes reported having an excellent relationship with their mother and 45 percent said they had an excellent relationship with their father. Of the teens who didn't regularly eat dinner with their family, only 36 percent reported having an excellent relationship with their mother and just 28 percent said they had an excellent relationship with their father. Family dinners make a difference!

Relationships take time to develop, even in our families. Start early on and establish family traditions, such as family mealtimes, when your baby is young.

Turn Off the Television

Preparation for family mealtime can start even before birth. A study by New York University School of Medicine found that mothers who often watched TV during mealtimes while they were pregnant were five times more likely to let their infants watch TV during mealtime when they were feeding.

It can be tempting to turn on the TV during mealtime, especially if it's just you and your baby. Try to resist the urge. If you let your child watch TV while he's eating as an infant or toddler, he won't want to turn the TV off during mealtime when he gets older. Plus, it's a distraction. Teach mindful eating. We can't listen to our body's cues of hunger and fullness when distracted by electronics. It's important for you to take the time to bond with your baby during mealtime and to keep the focus on learning to eat. Learning to eat is a new skill and it requires your baby's attention.

THIRTY-THREE PERCENT OF MOTHERS ADMIT THAT THEIR BABIES WERE EXPOSED TO TV DURING FEEDING.

According to research by the American Academy of Pediatrics, watching TV during meals is associated with a poorer quality diet and can lead to obesity later in life. TV watching makes it difficult for the child to self-feed and mothers often step in and help feed their child. The TV distracts both the parent and the child from being able to tell when the child is full, leading to poor self-regulatory skills.

The risk of obesity related to eating in front of the TV continues as children get older. Watching TV can lead to eating more food and eating a less nutritious diet. A study by the University of Minnesota found that boys who watch TV during family meals consumed fewer vegetables and grains and more sugar than those who did not watch TV. Girls ate fewer dark vegetables and more fried foods when eating in front of a TV.

Make Mealtime a Positive Event

From the beginning, make the decision that mealtime is going to be a positive event that your family can share together. You may want to start mealtime with a song or prayer to help structure the meal and signal that it's time for everyone to stop what he or she is doing and come together to eat at the table. This can help keep your kids seated at the table when they get old enough to get up and walk around.

Get in the habit of sharing your thoughts with your child. If it's just you and your baby at the table, and she's too young to talk, you can use this time to model good eating behavior. Talk about the characteristics of the foods your child is eating, using words like "crunchy" and "melt" or "savory" and "tart." Or tell your child a story, pausing to allow her to absorb the words. Babies understand more than we often give them credit for. You'll not only be helping your child understand the social aspects of the family table, but you'll also be working on language skills. If the entire family is at the table, it's beneficial for your baby to experience the conversations everyone else is having so she can join in with babbles and laughter and, when she's ready, with words.

Make Family Mealtime Work for You

While eating together at every meal is ideal, it's not always realistic in today's busy world. Parents often work late and brothers and sisters can have afterschool activities. Your goal should be to eat a meal together as a family five times per week—even if that meal is breakfast or lunch.

Choose what works for you. If mom or dad often works late, you may find that you eat dinner together Friday, Saturday, and Sunday evenings and then share brunch on Saturday and Sunday. If there are older siblings with sports activities that start at six, do an early dinner at 4 o'clock. The important thing is not which meal you share but that you spend time together, sharing in the eating experience on a regular basis.

Try These Mealtime Conversation Starters

Sharing in family mealtime will improve your child's communication skills and language development.

If your child is too young to talk:

- Use short statements, talking a bit slower and pausing for his reaction. Your baby is learning a new language and needs a few more seconds to process and respond to information.

- Tell stories about when you were a child and observe your child's response. You're teaching reciprocity.

- Share interesting news you learned today, no matter how simple or silly it is. Keep in mind that your baby is listening and responding in her own way, perhaps with a smile or a wide-eyed expression.

- Tell your child what is in the food he's eating, including the sounds it makes in our mouths (crunch!) and the way it feels (brrr . . . cold!) along with the taste (tart!).

- Point to foods and say their name, using fun and silly expressions, intonation, enthusiasm, and delight.

With early talkers:

- Play "I spy with my little eye," keeping it appropriate for their cognitive skill.

- Ask your child about her favorite game or toy.

- Play guess the ingredients in a meal. Even young kids can play a simplified version of this. Encourage them to use their eyes and other senses to discover ingredients.

For older children:

- Who is your favorite superhero? What superpowers would you like to have?

- What is your favorite sport and why? Talk about your favorite sport as a child too.

- Take turns creating a story and adding on different parts. It's a fantastic way to build memory skills.

- Ask what your child's favorite moment of the day was and why. What was a not-so-good moment? This popular "Roses and Thorns" game is a terrific way to gauge how your child is feeling.

Dining Out

Dining out can be a challenge with your little eater, but a fun change of pace, too. You'll encounter unfamiliar food choices, worries about cleanliness, fussiness, and the mess! Here are some tips to help you survive your next restaurant visit and make sure you'll look forward to going back again.

SKIP THE KID'S MENU

Kid's menus are typically filled with foods that society has deemed as kid's fare—chicken fingers, hot dogs, and fries. While these foods are okay for the occasional treat, you don't want your child to grow up associating these unhealthy food choices with dining out.

In most cases it's okay to share what you're eating with your child rather than ordering special kid's food. Be wary of tough meat and any other potential choking hazards, though.

You'll also need to take the salt content into consideration. Many restaurants go overboard on salt. This isn't healthy for adults, and too much salt can be dangerous for children. Mention to your server that you will be sharing your meal with your child and request that the kitchen prepare it without any added salt. Chances are some salt will still make its way into the meal, but your risk of overly high salt content will be much lower if you take this precaution.

Get the Most from Family Mealtime

- Family mealtime helps build a strong and lasting relationship with your child.
- Your baby should take part in family mealtime as soon as she starts to eat solid foods.
- Turn off the television during mealtime.
- Structure your mealtime and signal it's starting time with a song or prayer.
- Encourage your child to communicate with the family during mealtime.
- Aim to share a family meal five times a week.
- Make mealtimes work for you. You don't always need to eat dinner together at 5:00 p.m. What is important is that you share time together while enjoying healthy foods.
- The most important part of family mealtimes is family. It's about spending time together, not how many bites of food your child takes.
- Have fun!

HIGH CHAIR SAFETY

If you're using a restaurant high chair, don't trust that it has been cleaned properly prior to your visit. Even if it looks clean, it may have received only a quick wipe down to remove surface food. It may still harbor harmful bacteria such as *E. coli* and *Staphylococcus aureus*, which can only be removed with a disinfectant. In fact, a study of 30 American restaurants found that many restaurant high chairs contain more bacteria than public toilet seats. The study found that the average bacteria count found on restaurant highchairs was 147 per square centimeter, whereas toilet seats harbored an average of only 8 bacteria per square centimeter. While some high chairs were relatively clean, one restaurant's high chairs had a bacteria concentration of 1,200 per square centimeter!

If possible, bring your own portable high chair with a tray. Portable high chairs that clip onto tables are relatively small and easy to carry with you. Always carry disinfectant wipes and do a thorough wipe down of both the tray and the seat area prior to placing your child in the high chair.

Even once you've disinfected the tray or tabletop, you won't want to place your baby's food directly on the tray like you may do at home. Bring a bowl or plate with a suction base to place your child's food in. That way he can't toss the plate and food, but he will have a clean surface to eat off of. We like the Happy Mat by ezpz (ezpzfun.com). The partitioned plate is built right into the mat, keeping tabletop germs at bay and preventing plates from being tossed on the floor. Let's be real: At home, you might pick up a piece of food off the floor and declare the "five-second rule!" But I doubt you'll want to do the same in a restaurant.

Many restaurant high chairs offer minimal support, so carry a towel or blanket with you to roll up and place around your child's torso for added support and to boost stability. Here's a trick for those soft-bottomed booster seats that hook onto the side of the table: Hook them onto the table while a regular chair is pushed beneath the booster. Then, lay your purse or something flat and firm between the chair seat and the baby's bottom. When your child is seated in the booster, he'll now have something firm to sit on, yet be buckled in and safe in his soft-sided booster seat. Plus, if the restaurant chair is deep enough, he may even have a footrest, too. Instant stability!

HOW TO KEEP THE MESS TO A MINIMUM

We've encouraged you to let your child self-feed and to expect mess, but no one wants a child who is covered from head to toe with tomato sauce while they're at a restaurant. We encourage you to stick to foods that are easy to pick up, such as small pieces of fish, steamed veggies, bread, pasta with minimal sauce, and soft meats. Unless you're doing the feeding, avoid spoon-fed meals. Bring along a jar or pouch of puree for these occasions and be sure to engage your child, making the entire restaurant experience about your time together while enjoying the food.

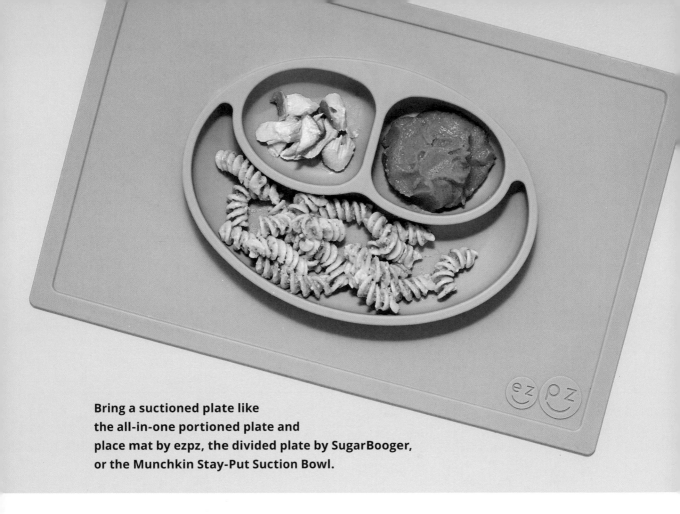

**Bring a suctioned plate like
the all-in-one portioned plate and
place mat by ezpz, the divided plate by SugarBooger,
or the Munchkin Stay-Put Suction Bowl.**

KEEP BABY HAPPY

Be respectful of other diners. No one wants an unhappy, fussy baby at the next table, nor will you enjoy your dining experience. While your child may be happy looking around at the new faces for a while, know that she will likely have a time limit on her attention span.

Order food quickly and don't let your child get too hungry. Have a snack that you know your baby likes, such as fruits or veggies, so that she can have a bite to eat while she's waiting for the meal to come. Ask the waiter for some orange slices or bread to bring out right away while waiting for the entree to arrive. Your waiter will be happy to oblige.

Bring an activity bag with a few little toys such as cars or animals, a book, and crayons with paper to keep your child entertained while you eat. Save these toys just for this purpose so that every time you pull them out of your bag, they have a special appeal to your child.

Dining Out Survival Kit

Carry the following items with you in your diaper bag to make dining out a smooth experience:

- Disinfectant wipes
- Towel or small blanket
- Portable high chair (optional)
- High chair cover if using the restaurant high chair (optional)
- Suction bowl and/or plate
- Small "special" toys
- Wipeable book
- Crayons and paper

Dining Out Success Secrets

- Skip the kid's menu.
- Let your child eat the same food you ordered, but request that your meal be made with less salt.
- Bring a portable high chair, if possible, or wipe down the restaurant high chair with disinfectant wipes. Consider a high chair cover.
- Bring a towel or small blanket for added stability when baby is seated.
- Place your child's food in a suctioned plate or bowl.
- Avoid high-mess foods.
- Order quickly. Request foods to nibble on like orange slices or bread while waiting for entrees to arrive. Bring a snack in case the meal takes a long time to arrive.
- Have activities to keep your child occupied.

CHAPTER 9

Addressing Picky Eating

Allowing your child to self-feed by offering a variety of healthy foods and allowing him to decide what to eat can go a long way toward preventing picky eating. Parents often find that the more they try to persuade their child to eat what they want, the higher the risk of that child becoming a fussy eater. Generally speaking, the earlier you offer a range of choices, encourage food exploration, and have consistent, reciprocal or social meals together while allowing your child to choose from the food you present, the better your chances of having an adventurous eater.

Continuing to spoon-feed your child once she has the desire and capability to feed herself can have a similar effect to a parent saying "finish all your vegetables before you leave the table" to an older child. It can make the child rebel against eating your chosen food or diminish her ability to self-regulate her food intake, leading to overeating.

LOWER LEVELS OF PARENTAL CONTROL WITH REGARDS TO A CHILD'S DIET ARE ASSOCIATED WITH LOWER LEVELS OF PICKINESS AND FUSSINESS IN CHILDREN.

Sometimes parents can encourage self-feeding from a young age, and feel that they're doing everything "right," and still wind up with a child who turns his nose up at almost every healthy food that is placed in front of him. If you're worried about your child's picky eating habits, here's a look at what to do and how to get help.

Avoid the Term "Picky Eater"

Never use the term *picky eater* in front of your child—even if she's too young to talk. Kids tend to live up to the labels we assign to them, so it's best not to brand your child as a picky eater.

Instead of focusing on what your child can't or won't eat, focus on what he can do with food. Celebrate the small accomplishments. If your baby is reluctant to pick up any vegetables and then one day, he begins to play with his peas, squishing them, exploring them, and perhaps even licking his fingers, then that is a big step! Join in the fun and play right along with him as your way of acknowledging his accomplishments. Kids want parents to join in. It has much more power than saying, "Good job licking the peas off your fingers." We encourage silly and fun ways to express your pleasure in your child's growing food exploration. Try a silly saying such as: "You squished the pea like a dinosaur goes stomp, stomp, stomp! You're a pea-stomping dinosaur!"

Adjust Your Child's Seating Position

Look at the way your child is positioned in her high chair. One of the most common reasons kids have difficulty eating is because they are positioned incorrectly at the table. Your baby should be seated in a secure position with her hips at slightly less than a 90-degree angle and her feet resting on a footrest for added stability.

A young child may also need additional stability around her hips in order to keep her trunk still while she's learning to eat finger foods. A rolled-up towel behind your child's back can provide the needed lumbar support, while also helping to stabilize the sides of her pelvis.

Model Good Eating Behavior

Model good table manners and eat with your child whenever possible. If it's mealtime for your child and you're not hungry, grab a glass of water and sit at the table facing your child. Try to avoid turning on the television so that your child can focus on learning about the new foods in front of him. If you limit distractions and keep the focus on food you'll increase the chances of your child wanting to explore and have fun with his food.

Avoid Pressure Tactics

It's common for bitter-tasting foods like vegetables to be initially rejected by young children. Avoid the urge to use pressure tactics to get your child to eat foods that he is pushing away. While it might get your child to eat that food temporarily, it most often backfires and can cause lasting, negative impressions about those foods. Remember, your goal is to raise a child who pays attention to his own hunger cues and sensory system. Gradual exposure over time as he grows is most effective. If your child is strongly opposed to a certain food, simply take the food away and reintroduce that particular item at another time.

Don't get discouraged. Some children may need to be exposed to different foods—especially some vegetables and fruits—a number of times before they establish their likes and dislikes. In fact, it's not uncommon for a child to need to try a food up to 16 times before accepting it.

Continue to offer a variety of healthy foods, without pressure, and most children will eventually come around. When your child does take a bite, offer positive affirmation for trying something new by talking about the characteristics of the food. For example, "That first bite of carrot was really crunchy and loud!" Kids love attention like that and we aren't trying to get them to eat carrots for us; we are trying to help them learn to try carrots for them. It's an autonomous decision.

DON'T FORCE YOUR CHILD TO EAT CERTAIN FOODS. YOUNG ADULTS REPORTED THAT THE FOODS THEY DISLIKE AS ADULTS WERE THOSE THAT THEY HAD BEEN COERCED TO EAT AS YOUNG CHILDREN.

Use Positive Reinforcement

If your child makes a big deal about not eating a food, the best thing you can do is give the act little to no attention. Compare learning to eat new foods to the toddler who stumbles and falls on the way to the park. That toddler can either choose to get back up and continue walking or she can cry out with loud, piercing wails.

While most of what initially happens will depend on the personality or sensory system of the kid who fell, much of the learned reaction—and what will happen when this same thing happens again and again in the future—is dependent on the parent's reaction to the fall, or more important, to the parent's response to the child's reaction. If after every dramatic sob, the child's mother rushes to scoop the child up and smoothers him with kisses, then the child is likely to be dramatic when he falls again in the future. He'll learn that if he is dramatic it yields lots of love and attention. If, however, the parent waited for the child to stand up and maybe offered a casual, "You're okay—I'll help brush off the dirt and we'll be off to the park," then the child learns to get back on his feet without all the tears and mayhem.

The same principles can be applied to learning to eat new foods. Reinforce the desired behavior, which at first may simply be picking up that long, wiggly string bean. That's the time to give your child some attention with a fun, engaging comment, such as "That string bean is soooo wiggly!" Responding to the undesired behavior (the string bean just sits on the plate) with "How about trying that green bean? It's really, really good! You'll like it!" is actually giving the behavior of *not* picking up the green bean quite a lot of attention. You are accidently reinforcing the child not touching the green bean. One of the most powerful things we can do as parents is present an opportunity and then wait.

There is a lot of power in waiting for a child to organize his sensory system, study the situation, and then act. Sometimes green beans just need to be the dinnertime science experiment. Try showing your child how to pop open the pod of the bean, exposing the "baby beans" inside. With time, as you model and talk about the characteristics of the food while tasting it—"Wow, that's saltier than I thought and it squeaks when I bite into it!"—kids will come around to trying it on their own. Your positive interactions, rather than your cheerleading, will make the biggest difference.

Take It Slow

If your child is adverse to new tastes and textures, then offering too many new foods at once can be overwhelming. Instead, present one new food along with familiar ones that your child is used to and already likes. If he fusses about it, be calm and concise and say matter-of-factly: "Yes, we all have broccoli on our plates today." Then, move on to a new topic. Say it once and don't revisit it. Just learning to accept the presence of a new food is a good first step.

Once your child gets comfortable with the new food on her plate you can share some cool facts about the new food, even with a three-year-old. For example: Did you know broccoli makes you super strong? Broccoli is Iron Man's favorite food. The average person eats over 4 pounds (1.8 kg) of broccoli a year! Making food fun will make it more appealing and your child will be more likely to take a bite.

Know When It's Time to Seek Help

No two kids are alike when it comes to learning to eat. For some children, exploring the world of food is a joyful experience, but for others it can be more complicated. There is a long list of reasons why a child may be averse to certain foods. And while many picky eating situations can be sorted out at home, there are times when parents should seek the help of a pediatrician or a feeding specialist.

If your child has not taken to any food by eight months of age, you should see a doctor to rule out any medical or developmental issues. What may appear to be just typical picky eating may have an underlying medical cause, such as constipation, sensory processing difficulties, gastroesophageal reflux disease, an undetected tongue-tie, or a motor delay. These are just a few examples of physiological, sensory, or motor challenges that can impact a child's behavior around food.

THE LINKS BETWEEN SPEECH AND FEEDING

There is often a correlation between speech and feeding issues. The act of feeding is complex and requires a great deal of versatility of movement from the mouth, jaw, tongue, and facial muscles. If a child is having trouble with speech due to low muscle tone and/or difficulties with the facial muscle movement that is required to talk, then those issues will often impact her eating as well. Sensory processing difficulties can also influence how a child develops speech, language, and feeding skills.

A visit to a speech-language pathologist (SLP) who specializes in feeding development can help determine whether your child's eating issues are related to speech difficulties or delays. If there is an issue, a speech therapist can offer solutions to get development back on the right track. Ask your child's pediatrician to refer you to a certified speech-language pathologist for any concerns around speech and language, especially if your child:

- Has not reached specific speech/language milestones, including early babbling
- Drools almost every day
- Appears frustrated when trying to communicate
- Struggles to communicate or is not understood by peers or unfamiliar listeners
- Appears unaware of sounds in his environment
- Is uncomfortable mouthing toys or never mouths toys

- Is highly resistant to tooth brushing
- Has begun to stutter (dysfluency)
- Has an unusual vocal quality or intonation to his voice
- Has a wet quality to his voice
- Coughs on a daily basis, especially when drinking or eating

Whether you see that your child is having difficulty with speech and language development or you have no concerns in that area, it's important to know the "red flags" for feeding difficulties. Red flags that your child's feeding skills may require some support from a specialist appear when your child:

- Has not reached specific feeding milestones
- Has not fully transitioned off only eating purees by nine months
- Has not learned to drink from a straw or open cup by 18 months
- Has not learned to use a spoon and fork independently by 18 months
- Has difficulty chewing and swallowing age-appropriate foods
- Coughs while eating
- Repeatedly gags while eating or when near food
- Has a highly sensitive sense of smell that impacts his willingness to try new foods
- Has a history of respiratory illnesses
- Has not learned to enjoy food or requires distraction while eating
- Has a limited repertoire of foods that she will eat
- Cannot eat in a variety of environments, including restaurants and school
- Is rigid about food in any way
- Becomes upset if new foods are presented on his plate
- Has nutritional deficits and/or poor growth

If the child's relationship with food influences the family's relationship with food, or family dynamics are focused on the child's "picky eating," then these are also issues of concern.

GASTROINTESTINAL ISSUES

If a child has persistent feeding issues, parents should consult with a pediatrician about possible gastrointestinal issues; the pediatrician may refer them to a pediatric gastroenterologist. If a child suffers from constipation, acid reflux, or pain in the abdominal region, it can create a negative association with eating and reluctance toward certain foods.

SENSORY SENSITIVITIES

Is your child a sensory seeker or a sensory avoider? Some children are averse to seeking out new sensory sensations and can quickly become overloaded if their body cannot process and organize a variety of sensory input. Ask yourself what sorts of tastes, temperatures, textures, auditory input (yes, every food has its own sound), and olfactory and visual stimuli your child tolerates, enjoys, resists, or avoids, especially when it comes to food. A feeding specialist can offer solutions to help your child explore new sensory food sensations as well as other sensory experiences she encounters on a day-to-day basis. Any concerns around sensory integration, which also includes the vestibular and proprioceptive systems, can be addressed by a registered pediatric occupational therapist (OT or OTR). If feeding is the primary issue, make sure the OT has experience in the assessment and treatment of feeding disorders.

MOTOR SKILL DELAYS

The development of gross and fine motor skills is directly related to how well a child will learn to bite, chew, and swallow a variety of foods. Motor delays can be due to a multitude of factors, including fluctuating, high, or low muscle tone; muscle weakness; and motor planning issues. If you observe signs of motor delays, please discuss your concerns with your pediatrician, who may refer your child for a physical or occupational therapy evaluation. Consult with a pediatrician if your child:

• Slumps in his high chair or requires extra support for sitting upright after eight months of age
• Feels floppy or too stiff in the trunk or extremities

- Has not reached specific motor milestones
- Appears uncoordinated
- Consistently favors one hand over the other before the age of three
- Favors one side of her body or one side appears weaker
- Has trouble with age-appropriate fine motor skills, such as grasping or using fingers for picking up objects
- Exhibits a regression in any motor skills

Solutions for Picky Eaters

- Encouraging both purees and self-feeding at a young age can boost your chances of having an adventurous eater.
- Avoid calling your child a picky eater. Try "food explorer" or "learning about eating" instead.
- Make sure your child is positioned correctly at the table with her torso supported, her hips and knees bent at about a 90-degree angle (anterior pelvic tilt), and her feet on a footrest.
- During mealtime, sit facing your child whenever possible.
- Keep distractions to a minimum so your child can focus on exploring his food.
- Accepting new foods can take time, but don't try to force your child to eat something he doesn't want to. Offer one new food at a time and give time for your child to taste it. If he doesn't, simply offer it again at another meal the next day or later in the week.
- A child may need to be exposed to a new taste many times before she accepts it.
- Don't overload your child with too many new tastes all at once. Offer one new food at time, along with familiar tastes that your child already likes.
- If you child has not taken to any food by eight months of age, you should see a doctor to rule out any medical or developmental issues, such as speech issues, low muscle tone, or developmental delays.

- CHAPTER 10 -
Recipes for Early Self-Feeders (6 to 9 Months)

Ah, the joy of having an early self-feeder! Although your baby may be interested in everything you eat, and it may seem as though she could just eat anything off of your plate, that won't be possible for quite some time. In practice, not all foods are soft enough or the right size for a baby to eat safely and effectively. While the goal of self-feeding is ultimately to create one family meal for everyone, you'll want to serve foods with a bit of a baby twist in the early months of self-feeding.

The following recipes have all been baby-tested for taste and ease of eating. They're also easy to prepare and good enough that mom, dad, and the rest of the family will be happy to eat them, too—even the purees can be used as a sandwich spread or a healthy addition to baking or pancakes. Get ready to explore the wonderful world of food with your baby.

Avocado Puree

Avocados are a healthy first food for your baby because they are rich in healthy monounsaturated fats and are a great source of vitamin E, a powerful antioxidant that boosts immunity. They are also high in calories, making them a healthful choice for a growing baby who is just learning to eat and needs to make every bite count.

1. Cut out a large slice of avocado and peel.

2. Mash the flesh in a bowl with a fork and mix in the milk for a smoother consistency.

3. Add the lemon juice to help maintain color and prevent browning.

YIELD: 2 SERVINGS

¼ avocado

1 teaspoon breast milk or formula

Squirt of fresh lemon juice

Self-Feeding Options

Once your baby starts self-feeding you can use this avacado puree as a healthy spread on toast or soft pita.

Spinach and Carrot Puree

Researchers have found that carrots are the most favored vegetable taste among infants, which makes carrots a healthy partner to help introduce other vegetables that have a more bitter taste, such as spinach. Popeye's favorite veggie is the ideal choice for infants, because it is high in iron and rich in vitamins A, C, and K. Spinach also contains glycoglycerolipids that help protect the gastrointestinal tract. Don't feel you have to limit yourself to one type of veggie per puree. Mix and match fruits and veggies for new flavor combinations and maximum nutritional benefits.

1. Preheat the oven to 375°F (190°C, or gas mark 5).

2. Cut the carrots into approximately 2-inch (5 cm) thick slices, place the spinach on top, and wrap the veggies in tinfoil.

3. Place on the center rack and cook for approximately 30 minutes, or until the carrots are soft.

4. Allow to cool and then place in a blender with a little breast milk, formula, or water. Blend until smooth.

YIELD: 6 SERVINGS

2 carrots, peeled

2 cups (140 g) spinach, washed

2 tablespoons (30 ml) breast milk, formula, or water

Save It for Later

This puree freezes well. Try placing in ice cube trays to freeze so you can thaw individual servings later.

Sweet Potato Fries

These fries are the perfect size for babies to hold. By substituting nutrient-rich sweet potatoes for traditional potatoes, you give this side dish a healthy makeover. Sweet potatoes are one of the best sources of beta-carotene. Plus, several studies have shown that sweet potatoes have a superior ability to raise vitamin A levels, especially in children.

1. Preheat the oven to 400°F (200°C, or gas mark 6).

2. Peel the potatoes and cut into lengthwise strips about the width of your finger.

3. Place in a large bowl and toss with the oil and cinnamon.

4. Spread onto a baking sheet and bake for 25 to 30 minutes (turning once), or until tender.

YIELD: 4 SERVINGS

2 sweet potatoes

1 tablespoon (15 ml) olive oil

1 teaspoon ground cinnamon (optional)

Healthy Substitutions

Try substituting parsnips or butternut squash for the sweet potatoes.

Panko-Crusted Baked Veggies

When your child is just learning to pick up food, slippery surfaces can be tough for her to grasp. By covering veggie sticks in a crusted coating, you make them easier to pick up and create a texture that is easier for your baby to feel and move around in her mouth.

1. Preheat the oven to 400°F (200°C, or gas mark 6).

2. Whisk the warm water and flaxseed in a shallow bowl and add a pinch of salt; set aside.

3. Peel the veggies, if necessary, and cut into long strips about the width of your finger. Spray a cookie sheet with oil and place at the end of the counter.

4. Place the panko crumbs on a plate and set the plate beside the flax mixture. Roll each piece of veggie in the flaxseed mixture and then roll in the panko crumbs. Place on the cookie sheet.

5. Bake for about 25 minutes, flipping once. Veggies should be tender and golden brown on the outside when finished.

YIELD: 4 SERVINGS

3 tablespoons (45 ml) warm water

1 tablespoon (15 ml) ground flaxseed

Pinch of salt

About 1 pound (455 g) veggies (sweet potatoes, parsnips, carrots, zucchini, and eggplant all work well)

Spray cooking oil

1 cup (50 g) panko crumbs

Mix Master

Don't feel you need to stick to one type of veggie. Eating a colorful variety of vegetables is the best way to get your fill of nutrients. Carrots and sweet potatoes are rich in vitamin A and beta-carotene. Zucchini is rich in vitamin C and eggplant has a unique phytonutrient, nasunin, which helps protect cell membranes from damage.

Zucchini French Toast

This is a healthy breakfast for the whole family. The French toast also freezes well, so you can cook extra and then pop a slice in the toaster to serve for breakfast at a later date.

1. Make your own zucchini puree by cutting the zucchini into 2-inch (5 cm) pieces and steaming for about 5 minutes, or until soft. Add to a blender and blend until smooth, adding water, 1 tablespoon (15 ml) at a time, if needed. You can make puree ahead and freeze so that you have it on hand. Measure out ¼ cup (30 g) for the recipe.

2. Crack the eggs into a wide dish and whisk. Add the zucchini puree, milk, and cinnamon and then whisk to combine.

3. Heat a frying pan over medium heat and spray with olive oil cooking spray.

4. Dip the bread into mixture for about 2 seconds on each side or until thoroughly coated. Place in the pan and cook until each side is browned, 3 to 4 minutes.

5. Cut into strips and serve with a side dish of vanilla yogurt or maple syrup for dipping, if desired.

YIELD: 6 SLICES

1 zucchini

5 eggs

2 tablespoons (30 ml) milk

1 teaspoon ground cinnamon

Olive oil cooking spray

6 slices whole-grain bread

Dairy-Free Option

You can skip milk by using an extra 2 tablespoons (15 g) zucchini puree.

Cuban-Style Oatmeal

You can add soft beans to oatmeal as a way to increase iron in your baby's diet. This Cuban-inspired dish is a creative way to turn a traditional breakfast into an iron-fortified lunch or dinner.

1. Bring the water to a boil in a saucepan over high heat.

2. Add the oats, stir, and reduce the heat to low. Simmer for 30 minutes, stirring occasionally.

3. Heat the olive oil in a frying pan over medium heat. Cook the plantains until golden brown, about 2 minutes per side.

4. Place the oats in a bowl and top with a scoop of beans, plantains, and avocado slices.

YIELD: 4 SERVINGS

4 cups (910 ml) water

1 cup (80 g) steel-cut oats

1 tablespoon (15 ml) olive oil

2 ripe plantains, cut into small cubes

1 can (15 ounces, or 420 g) black beans, rinsed, drained, and patted dry

1 ripe avocado, peeled and cut into small cubes

Short on Time?

Substitute quick or instant oats for steel-cut.

Tomato Sauce

Most store-bought tomato sauces are high in added sugar. Feeding them to your child from an early age may encourage cravings for sweet foods. Making your own tomato sauce is simple and much healthier, and it can be frozen to serve at a later date. It not only goes well with pasta but is also a delicious topping or dipping sauce for cooked veggies.

1. Heat the olive oil in a saucepan over low heat. Add the garlic and cook until browned, about 3 minutes.

2. Add the basil and tomatoes with juice. Turn the heat to high and bring the sauce to a boil.

3. Once boiling, turn the heat down to low and simmer for 40 minutes, stirring occasionally and crushing the tomatoes with the back of a spoon.

4. Add a pinch of salt and pepper to season, let cool, and serve.

YIELD: 2 CUPS (500 G)

1 tablespoon (15 ml) extra virgin olive oil

2 cloves garlic, mashed

2 fresh basil leaves, finely diced

1 can (28 ounces, or 784 g) whole peeled tomatoes with juice

Pinch of sea salt and pepper

Fresh Appeal

Substitute 10 to 12 fresh tomatoes (depending on size) for canned. Peel and deseed prior to cooking.

Stew with Soft Meat

It's important to introduce meat to your baby at around six to eight months of age. Your baby won't have many teeth at this age, and she is just learning to chew, so choose a meat that is soft. Stewed beef is an ideal first meat because the extended cooking time softens the meat. Even though this meat is tender, be sure to cut it into pea-size cubes before giving it to your baby. Short on time? You can cook the meat the night before and refrigerate.

1. Cut the beef into 2-inch (5 cm) cubes. (You can cut it smaller for your child once the beef is cooked.) Heat the oil and 1 tablespoon (14 g) of the butter over medium heat in a large saucepan and brown the meat for about 4 minutes on each side. Remove from the pan and set aside.

2. Add the remaining 2 tablespoons (28 g) butter to the saucepan and sauté the chopped onions until tender and golden, about 5 minutes. Stir in the flour and continue cooking for another 2 or 3 minutes.

3. Return the meat to the saucepan and add the seasonings and water. Simmer, partially covered, until the beef is tender, about 90 minutes.

4. While the beef is cooking, peel the sweet potatoes, onions, carrots, and parsnips and cut into 1- to 2-inch (2.5 to 5 cm) cubes. Core and seed the peppers and cut into squares.

5. Once the meat has cooked for at least 90 minutes, add the veggies and canned tomatoes and cook for another 30 or 40 minutes, adding more water (¼ cup [60 ml] at a time) if necessary.

YIELD: 8 SERVINGS

2 ½ pounds (1 kg) lean boneless stew beef

2 tablespoons (30 ml) olive oil

3 tablespoons (42 g) unsalted butter, divided

¾ cup (120 g) finely chopped onions

¼ cup (30 g) flour

1 teaspoon dried basil

½ teaspoon dried oregano

¼ teaspoon dried rosemary

½ teaspoon dried parsley

¼ teaspoon salt

½ teaspoon black pepper

½ teaspoon celery seed

1 tablespoon (6 g) onion powder

4 cups (910 ml) water

4 sweet potatoes

4 onions

4 parsnips

8 carrots

4 green or red bell peppers

2 cans (28 ounces, or 784 g each) whole tomatoes, including liquid

CHAPTER 11

Recipes for Emergent Self-Feeders (10 to 12 months)

Get ready for an adventurous little eater! From six to nine months of age your child was working on building his trunk stability. Now at this stage, she can sit with limited support and for longer periods and, because of this added stability, she's ready to really have fun with her food!

By about nine months, your baby was also beginning to figure out how to control her jaw, mouth, and tongue—both individually and together. Now her intentions are more purposeful. She is getting better at picking up tiny pieces of food, too. Your baby is developing a full pincer grasp and is likely starting to pick items up with the side of her thumb or the tip and side of her middle or pointer finger. With all of these new skills, your baby is ready to explore and really start having some fun with her food!

Encourage pincer grasp development by offering round cereal or pea-size pieces of soft food in the following ways:

1 Take a plastic "shot glass" or similar sized narrow container (about 2 inches [5 cm] tall and just wide enough for your child's thumb and forefinger to grasp). Put a few pieces of cereal in the bottom and encourage your child to get them out by reaching in and picking up the pieces using her pincer grasp.

2 Take a round plastic coffee stirrer and thread onto it three pieces of circular cereal (such as Cheerios). Hold the stir stick perpendicular to the high chair tray and let your child pull off the cereal pieces one by one using his thumb and forefinger.

3 When giving your child a piece of food, hold it in your pincer grasp, with half the food sticking out and available for your baby's little fingers to grab on to. Let your child take the food from your grasp and put it in her mouth.

Changes in an Emergent Diet

As your baby masters new feeding skills, meal frequency will increase with the goal of your baby eating three solid meals by the time he's 12 months old. Babies tend to like the food that they grow accustomed to, so it's important to introduce as many different, healthy foods as possible during this time period. Babies who like a varied diet tend to turn into children who enjoy a variety of foods.

Focus on fruits and vegetables; whole-grain breads, pastas, and other starches; proteins such as meat, fish, eggs, beans, and tofu; and dairy products such as yogurt, cheese, and even a bit of milk. Although babies can handle some cow's milk prior to one year of age, experts say it shouldn't be a dominant source of liquid in your child's diet for the first year of life. Your baby still needs the added nutrients from breast milk or formula during this time, so most of her fluids will continue to come from one of these sources. However, you will notice that breast or bottle feedings gradually start to taper off as your baby eats more and more solid foods, and your child may drop a feeding or two during this emergent eater phase.

Explore Tastes and Textures

It's important to feed your baby as many different tastes and textures as possible; just keep your choices healthy and safe. While your baby may be able to handle slightly larger pieces of soft foods—kidney bean size rather than pea size—his windpipe is relatively the same size as it was at six months. That means his windpipe (trachea) is about the same diameter as his finger. That's pretty narrow! In terms of choking hazards, foods still need to be small enough that they won't cause an obstruction.

Offer soft foods. Your baby's chewing skills will be improved, so she will be able to handle slightly firmer foods; however, you still don't want to offer anything as hard as a thick apple slice. It's the difference between a really ripe piece of avocado and a slightly firmer, but still ripe, piece of avocado.

Oily fish are a healthy choice during this age period because of the health benefits and the "slip factor" that makes them easy to swallow. You can also try making a variety of energy balls with mixed textures. Crushed nuts and very small seeds are fine. Make the balls at least the size of a golf ball so that your child can hold the food in his fist and bite off pieces for chewing. Always keep an eye on your child!

When you're thinking of new textures for your baby, don't forget about purees. Purees should remain part of your baby's food repertoire during this feeding stage, with the goal of feeding your child purees about three times a week. This doesn't mean you are spoon-feeding your baby purees, however. Let your baby get dirty and do the work for herself—at least to start. If your child gets discouraged, you can help her out at the end of the meal.

Purees are building blocks to better feeding control. They lead to better spoon use and eventually to using a fork. We essentially keep eating purees for the rest of our life at some level. Think about the last time you had soup or a smoothie! When your baby is just learning to eat with a spoon, slightly chunkier purees are easier for him to manage than a thin soup. Let your baby practice his self-feeding skills with purees that stick a bit to a spoon or to a dipper, as described in the next section.

Eating with a Spoon

During this phase your child will be able to locate a bowl with her hands. Babies will be able to grasp on to a spoon with a fat handle or even a stalk of soft broccoli and dip it into a puree or yogurt and eat it. Dipping is the first step to learning to use a spoon.

Your baby will be eating off a small, flat spoon with a fat handle at the beginning of this phase of learning to use a spoon. As he learns to suck food from a flat spoon, and his mouth begins to grow, he'll be ready for a slightly bigger spoon-bowl and one that is just a tad deeper. This will typically come around eight or nine months, depending on the size of your baby.

Be sure to keep using a spoon that has a fat handle, as it's easier for little fists to grasp firmly. The spoon handle should be short so that your child does not need to rotate his wrist very much as he brings the spoon up to his mouth. The closer his fist is to the end of the spoon, the easier it will be to go from dipping the spoon into a bowl of yogurt to bringing it to his mouth. If the short handle has a curve to it, then his fist should be holding the center of the handle. Longer handles on spoons are for the adult to hold the spoon comfortably while spoon-feeding and aren't ideal for little hands. If you do hand your baby a long-handled spoon, be sure to help him hold the handle as close to the bowl of the spoon as possible without dipping his fist into the food, too. To encourage your child to hold the spoon close to the spoon-bowl, try drawing a circle around the handle to give your baby a consistent spot to grab. Draw the circle about 1 inch (2.5 cm) from the spoon-bowl or, if the handle is curved, have him grasp the spoon at the top of the curve.

Your child's feeding bowl shouldn't be too far away from her mouth. The ideal tray height is one where your baby can rest her elbows on the tray to aid in spoon-feeding. This will give her better control over dipping the spoon into the food and putting it in her mouth. Suction bowls are also useful so that your baby won't pick the bowl up and throw it to get a reaction. Plus, suction bowls won't slide across the table as she learns to dip and scoop.

Drinking Through a Straw

Around nine months of age your baby can start to use a straw, and some babies can learn sooner than that. In fact, most seven-month-olds can learn to drink from a straw, but they will have trouble holding the cup and drinking from the straw at the same time. You'll have to hold the cup for them. By nine months, straw drinking is a breeze.

A straw is an effective way to let your baby self-feed with purees—adults drink purees all the time when enjoying thick kefirs, smoothies, and even piña coladas. Teach your baby to drink through a straw with purees before introducing thin liquids. It's actually easier for your baby to learn to sip purees through a straw than it is to learn to sip liquids because her tongue can hold the bolus of puree easily and it will slide right down her throat with ease. Thin liquids like water are more challenging to control at first.

Sipping purees through a straw is easier than self-feeding with a spoon, and your baby will be able to get more nutrients with less effort. However, the first step to learning to drink from a straw is learning to suck purees off fingers, spoons, or foods like a steamed carrot. The trick is to start with a smooth puree that your baby loves—applesauce and kefir are healthy choices. Put the puree in a small, short cup. Dip a firm-sided straw (average soda-shop diameter—not too thin, not too wide), cut down to about 6 inches (15 cm) long, into the puree, and present the straw to your baby, just as you would if you were using a spoon. There will be puree on the outside of the straw, just like a spoon, and your baby will open, close, and suck the puree off, just like it's a spoon.

Once your baby is finished, dip the straw in the puree again. This time cover the other end of the straw with a finger, so that about ½ inch (3 cm) of puree stays in the straw. Offer the straw to your baby in the same manner you did before, but wait one second after your baby closes her lips on the straw before you remove it. During this pause, you'll see your baby suck the puree out of the straw. Be sure to only have a very small amount of puree inside the straw so as not to startle her with a flood of food. Repeat this several times to ensure your baby's comfort.

When your child is comfortable sipping a small amount of puree out of the end of the straw, it's time to prime the straw by sucking on one end as it's dipped into the puree, and drawing up 2 inches (5 cm) of puree. Offer the straw as you did before, with your finger on the end of the straw, and allow your baby to suck the puree out of the end of the straw. Watch as your baby sucks, swallows, and repeats until the straw is empty. Then remove the straw from your baby's mouth.

Now, place the straw in a cup that is filled with puree. Prime the straw, filling it with puree. Then, use your clean finger to put a dab of puree on the top of the straw just before offering the cup and straw to your baby. That dab of puree will alert your child's taste buds and he'll begin to suck the straw. Soon he'll begin to suck puree up the straw all on his own. Over time, you won't have to prime the straw anymore, provided the cup is quite full and the straw is short. Just dab some puree on the tip of the straw and your baby will prime the food through the straw all on his own.

Within a few days of practicing, you'll no longer need the puree on the outside of the straw. Your child will know what to do when she sees the cup and straw. Keeping the cup full at first will facilitate learning the process and make the experience easy and enjoyable.

Slowly begin to water down the puree until your baby is drinking a thin liquid with ease. If you observe coughing, wincing, or any signs of discomfort, go back to thicker purees via the straw for a while. Most kids go from starting to drink purees through a straw to drinking water through a straw in about two weeks at the most. Once your baby can drink fluids through a straw, continue to offer purees through a straw around

Limit Food from Pouches

Although pouches are convenient and fine for occasional use, we discourage using them on a daily basis. Feeding is a reciprocal, social experience and pouches are not often the best match for interactive mealtime experiences. When offering your child a pouch, remember to engage and interact with him, just as you would while enjoying any food together. Kids sometimes suck away at a pouch and, almost without realizing it, suck down over 3 ounces (84 g) of fruit in a matter of minutes. That quick rush of fructose can stop the appetite for other foods, thanks to the sugar being absorbed so quickly.

three times a week. Using a straw will keep your baby's texture and taste repertoire as complex as possible. Remember, purees aren't necessarily from a jar. A smoothie is a puree, too! A thick soup or even a well-blended gazpacho is a puree.

Most important, never replace pouch feeding for other eating experiences. Melanie often sees little clients who *only* know how to suck from a pouch and never experience food and finger feeding. They easily grow accustomed to the quick, satisfying meals, forgoing the social experience of sitting at the table and interacting with family members. Or they are used to being handed vegetable and fruit pouches while riding in their car seats, because their parents just want to be sure their child got some decent nutrition every day. Kids can truly develop a "pouch habit" just as they can become dependent on juice boxes and sippy cups. Occasional use is fine, but focus on mealtimes together as a family above all else.

Let There Be Mess!

Although there will be times when you want to keep the mess to a minimum, let your baby get messy! Melanie says she always turns up her radar when she sees a baby sitting in her high chair, being fed by a caregiver and the baby is spotless. Well-meaning parents try to spare their child (and themselves) the mess associated with early eating by continuing to spoon-feed their little ones and offering only mess-free finger foods like rice puffs and Cheerios. Not only is the mess a vital part of the learning curve for self-feeding, but it's also essential for children to encounter the sensory experience of every food they eat. Children need to first explore new foods with their eyes, ears, nose, and hands before putting it in their mouths. As they do, they create memories of those experiences in their brains, comparing those memories to new encounters as they grow.

Mess is an important part of your baby's development, so don't shy away from it. Cover the floor with a washable mat to make cleaning up easier and let your baby have fun!

Tips for Emergent Eaters

- The goal is to have your child eating three meals a day by the time she's 12 months old.

- Continue to offer breast milk or formula until at least 12 months.

- Offer a variety of tastes and textures. Babies who like a varied diet turn into children who enjoy a variety of foods.

- Encourage your baby to explore and improve his pincer grasp.

- Your baby may be able to handle slightly larger pieces of food—kidney bean size rather than pea size. Just remember that your baby's windpipe is about the same size as it was at six months.

- Purees are building blocks to better feeding control. Your child should self-feed with purees on a spoon or through a straw about three times a week.

- Use a short, fat-handled spoon that is easy for your baby to grasp.

- Teach your baby to use a straw with purees, moving to liquids gradually over the course of two weeks.

- Get messy! Mess is part of the learning curve for self-feeding. It's essential for your child to enjoy a sensory experience when she eats.

Butternut Squash Puree

Purees play a role in your baby's diet even after she starts to eat finger foods. Let your child self-feed with a spoon, or even her fingers, or put puree in a cup and let your baby drink it through a straw. It's actually easier for your baby to drink purees than it is for her to drink liquids, so purees will help her learn to use a straw.

Combine all the ingredients in a high-speed blender and blend until smooth. Serve in a cup with a straw or let your baby self-feed with a spoon.

YIELD: 4 SERVINGS

1 cup (250 g) cooked, diced butternut squash

2 tablespoons (30 ml) water

½ teaspoon ground cinnamon

¼ teaspoon ground cumin

Dress It for Mom and Dad

Vegetables can make a terrific base for a salad dressing. Separate half of the puree and add 2 teaspoons (10 ml) olive oil and 1 teaspoon (5 ml) soy sauce for a tasty and healthy salad dressing that you can pour over your greens while your baby eats.

Brain Booster Smoothie

If you mix spinach into smoothies it doesn't change the taste, making it an effective way for anyone to get his or her daily fill of greens. Plus, the flaxseeds add brain-boosting omega-3 fatty acids. If your child doesn't finish the entire smoothie in one feeding, you can save it for a day in the refrigerator. Note: If you use fresh produce instead of frozen, add two or three ice cubes.

1. Combine all the ingredients in a high-speed blender and blend until smooth.

2. If the smoothie is too thick, add water 1 tablespoon (15 ml) at a time until you reach the desired consistency.

YIELD: 1 SMOOTHIE (APPROXIMATELY 1 CUP [235 ML])

½ cup (120 ml) whole milk

¼ cup (60 g) plain yogurt

½ banana, frozen or fresh

½ cup (35 g) spinach, frozen or fresh

2 teaspoons (10 g) peanut butter (optional)

½ tablespoon (7 g) flaxseeds

¼ teaspoon vanilla extract

⅛ teaspoon ground cinnamon

Freeze It for Later

Many people don't know that you can buy a bag of prewashed spinach and store it in your freezer. You always have it on hand and can just toss the frozen greens into your smoothie.

Broccoli Bites

Nancy swears by these broccoli bites. Each bite is packed with protein and vitamins and they're easy for your baby to grasp and eat on his own.

1. Preheat the oven to 375°F (190°C, or gas mark 5). Grease a baking sheet with butter.

2. Mix all the ingredients in a large bowl. Make into 12 small patties about the size of your palm and place on the baking sheet.

3. Cook for about 25 minutes, or until golden brown, flipping halfway through.

YIELD: 12 BITES

Unsalted butter,
 for greasing pan

2 cups (150 g) finely chopped steamed broccoli

1½ cups (180 g) grated cheddar cheese

3 eggs

1 cup (80 g) bread crumbs (pea-size)

Try It as a First Food

You can adapt this recipe for kids as young as six months by cutting broccoli into tinier pieces and using five egg yolks instead of the whole egg.

Banana Bread

Banana bread is an easy snack that you can take anywhere. This bread gets an added health boost with coconut oil and Greek yogurt.

1. Preheat oven to 325°F (160°C, or gas mark 3).

2. In a large bowl, whisk together the flour, baking soda, cinnamon, and salt. Set aside.

3. In a medium bowl, beat together the sugar and eggs for about five minutes, then drizzle in the melted coconut oil.

4. Add the bananas, yogurt, and vanilla. Mix just until combined.

5. Fold the wet mixture into the flour mixture.

6. Pour the batter into a non-stick 9-inch (23 cm) loaf pan and bake for an hour, or until the center springs back up when touched.

YIELD: ONE 9-INCH (23 CM) LOAF

1½ cups (188 g) flour

1 teaspoon baking soda

¼ teaspoon cinnamon

½ teaspoon sea salt

½ cup (113 g) brown sugar

2 eggs

½ cup (109 g) coconut oil, melted

3 large ripe bananas, mashed

3 tablespoons (45 g) Plain Greek yogurt

1 teaspoon vanilla extract

Energy Balls

In Melanie's book *Raising a Healthy, Happy Eater*, she and her co-author Nimali "Doctor Yum" Fernando created a variety of energy balls for all age groups to enjoy. Melanie has customized this recipe for emergent self-feeders, ensuring that ingredients are safe for these little food explorers.

1. Combine coconut flakes and pumpkin seeds in food processor and pulse to chop finely. Pour mixture into bowl, combining with 1 cup (80 g) rolled oats.

2. Add all the remaining ingredients to a food processor or blender and pulse until smooth.

3. Add to the oat mixture and stir until well mixed. Cover and refrigerate for 30 minutes; a cooler mixture is easier to work with.

4. Take the mixture from the fridge and use a melon baller or small spoon to scoop dough and then roll it into 1-inch (2.5 cm) balls. If your child tends to stuff this sized piece in his mouth, make the balls twice as large, so that he learns to bite off a piece and not stuff.

5. Roll each ball in the reserved oats to ensure that they are easy for little fingers to pick up.

6. Place balls in a glass container and store covered in the refrigerator for up to 2 weeks.

YIELD: 24 ENERGY BALLS

1 cup (80 g) rolled oats plus ½ cup (40 g) for coating the balls

1 cup (80 g) finely chopped coconut flakes

1 cup (80 g) finely chopped pumpkin seeds

1 cup (80 g) chopped dates

¼ cup (60 ml) brown rice syrup

¼ cup (60 ml) canned pumpkin (no added spices)

1 tablespoon (12 g) ground flaxseeds

1 teaspoon ground cinnamon

½ teaspoon ground ginger

½ teaspoon nutmeg

½ teaspoon salt

Veggie Substitutes

Sweet potato or butternut squash purees are a smart, fresh alternative to canned pumpkin.

Lemon Basil Hummus

This refreshing hummus is created by Nimali Fernando, a pediatrician and founder of The Doctor Yum Project based in Spotsylvania, Virginia. She founded Yum Pediatrics, which focuses on creating wellness through a healthy diet, as well as DoctorYum.org. This hummus is easy to spread on toast or use as a dip for soft or steamed veggies. It's packed with protein and easy for your baby to eat.

1. In a blender or food processor, blend all the ingredients (except the chickpea juice) until smooth.

2. If the consistency is too thick, add liquid a ¼ cup (60 ml) at a time until the desired thickness is achieved.

YIELD: ABOUT 2 CUPS (500 G)

2 cups (500 g) chickpeas (save liquid)

1 clove garlic

Juice and zest of 1 lemon

10 basil leaves

2 tablespoons (25 g) tahini or peanut butter

2 tablespoons (30 ml) olive oil

¼ teaspoon salt

Dash of black pepper

Choose Canned

Doctor Yum says that canned chickpeas work better than the dried, cooked version. Her favorite brand is Eden Organic because the lining in their cans is BPA-free and there's no added salt.

Pasta with Creamy Avocado Sauce

This ultra-healthy, creamy pasta sauce is like Alfredo but with avocado instead of cream, making it delicious *and* healthy.

1. Bring a large pot of salted water to a boil over high heat and cook the pasta according to package directions.

2. While the pasta is cooking, combine the basil and garlic in a food processor or blender and pulse to mince. Add the avocado, lemon juice, olive oil, water, salt, and pepper and blend until smooth.

3. When the pasta is cooked, drain and place back in the pot. Add the avocado sauce, stir to blend, and serve.

YIELD: 4 SERVINGS

1 cup (110 g) favorite uncooked pasta

¼ cup (12 g) fresh basil leaves

1 clove garlic

1 avocado, peeled and pitted

2 tablespoons (30 ml) fresh lemon juice

1 tablespoon (15 ml) olive oil

2 tablespoons (30 ml) water

¼ teaspoon salt

¼ teaspoon pepper

Just Add Fusilli

You can use any type of pasta, but fusilli is ideal for little eaters. The spirals in the pasta hold just the right amount of sauce in place, and are easier to grab.

Crust-Free Mini Quiche

Quiche is a healthy baby food because the consistency is easy for little ones to chew on and it is packed with protein and veggies.

1. Preheat the oven to 325°F (160°C, or gas mark 3). Grease mini muffin tins with butter and set aside.

2. Combine all the ingredients in a food processor or blender and pulse until the vegetables are in tiny pieces.

3. Pour the mixture into the muffin cups, filling each cup about three-fourths full. Bake for 25 minutes, or until golden brown and cooked throughout. Cool and serve.

YIELD: 12 MINI QUICHE

Unsalted butter, for greasing pan

2 eggs

⅓ cup (40 g) shredded cheddar cheese

½ cup (35 g) spinach

1 small zucchini, cut into slices

¼ cup (60 g) cottage cheese

¼ cup (60 ml) whole milk

Roasted Halibut with Orange, Artichoke, and Olive Salad

Chef and mom of two Tonia Wilson (toniawilson.com) found that her kids loved the citrus flavor of this fish recipe and it's a great way for the whole family to share a meal and get their fill of omega-3 fatty acids.

1. Preheat the oven to 350°F (180°C, or gas mark 4). Spray a baking sheet with oil.

2. Season the halibut fillets with salt and pepper and sprinkle each with ground coriander.

3. In a small bowl, stir together the mint, orange segments, artichokes, olives, and 2 tablespoons (30 ml) of the olive oil. Season with salt to taste and set aside.

4. In a large nonstick skillet, heat the remaining 2 tablespoons (30 ml) oil over medium-high heat. Gently place the fish in the oil and sear until golden on each side, about 8 minutes per side. Place the seared fish on the baking sheet (or keep in pan if it is ovenproof) and bake until the fish is just cooked through, about 8 minutes depending on thickness.

5. Divide the orange salad among 4 plates and top each with a piece of halibut. Cut baby's food into appropriate sizes. Chop orange segments and artichokes into smaller pieces if your baby isn't quite ready for a whole segment.

YIELD: 4 FAMILY-SIZE SERVINGS, OR 10 SERVINGS FOR BABY

Cooking oil spray

4 (5-ounce, or 140 g) skinless halibut fillets

Salt and freshly ground pepper to taste

1 teaspoon ground coriander

1 tablespoon (3 g) chopped fresh mint

1 orange, peeled and cut into segments

1 small bottle (6 ounces, or 180 g) artichoke quarters, drained

¼ cup (25 g) coarsely chopped pitted kalamata olives

4 tablespoons (60 ml) olive oil, divided

- CHAPTER 12 -
Recipes for Competent Self-Feeders (13 to 18 months)

Nice work! Your baby is starting to master the basics of eating on her own. She's also moving around more, and with walking comes increased trunk stability that will help her out at the table and give her more confidence when exploring food.

Since your child is becoming a more efficient eater, she can eat more food, at a faster rate. By 12 months she should be eating three meals a day and one or two snacks. If your child is on formula, she can transition to cow's milk at this time. If you choose to continue breastfeeding beyond a year, that's great, too. Just ensure that breast milk isn't taking the place of one of your child's three daily meals.

BY 18 MONTHS OF AGE, ABOUT 80 PERCENT OF A CHILD'S ENERGY INTAKE WILL COME FROM TABLE FOODS.

If your child is not quite able to feed herself independently by 12 months and still needs a little help, don't stress, but be sure to discuss it with her doctor, who may refer you to a feeding therapist to boost along her skills and offers tips for you to support her feeding development. Keep in mind that self-spoon feeding and using utensils will not be perfected until age two, but by age one children show an interest in using utensils. Every kid is different, and there are a lot of factors, including developmental rates and your child's temperament, that will determine the rate at which your child can self-feed with competency. Continue to take things slow and help out when needed and chances are your child will be self-feeding in a few months.

Your child's diet will continue to be a mixture of soft finger foods, handheld foods, chopped foods, and purees. Her chewing skills are improving, and a few more teeth are starting to peek through, so your child will be able to handle slightly harder foods. That doesn't mean she's ready for you to pass her a whole apple just yet. It's the difference between steamed vegetables and blanched vegetables. Hard foods that snap off in the mouth are not an option at this time.

Your child will now have a few front teeth to help break up food, and he may even see his first lower molars by about a year. That being said, he won't have a full set of molars until about 24 months. Even after that time, your child will need practice grinding up food. Choking risks are still high between one and three years of age, so you need to continue to watch for large chunks of food that may come off in your child's mouth and remember to never take your eyes off him when he's eating.

Your Child's Diet

Your baby is now eating three meals a day, plus healthy snacks. Although it's just a rough guideline, you should aim to feed your baby three or four servings of whole grains; three or four servings of fruit and vegetables; and two servings of protein, such as meat, fish, eggs, beans, tofu, or lentils. Your baby will also be getting about three daily servings of dairy products and/or breast milk.

BREAST MILK AND DAIRY

One of the most significant dietary changes at 12 months is the move away from formula. Your competent eater will be able to get enough nutrients through food by this age and she will be able to move from formula to cow or goat's milk as her primary source of liquid. Milk is a great source of calcium and vitamin D, and the American Academy of Pediatrics suggests 16 to 20 ounces (470 to 600 ml) of whole cow's milk a day between the ages of one and two. Drinking more than that may cause your child to fill up on milk and not get enough varied nutrients through food. Remember that calcium need not come from milk alone. Less milk is fine if your child is getting the same nutrition from cheese, leafy greens, soy, yogurt, chia seeds, or other calcium sources.

If you are breastfeeding, the choice is up to you whether you would like to continue. There are continued benefits to breastfeeding beyond the first year. Breast milk is packed with nutrients and will continue to boost your child's immunity. "Some immune factors in breast milk that protect the baby against infection are present in even greater amounts in the second year of life than in the first," says Dr. Jack Newman. "This is because children older than a year are generally exposed to more infections than young babies." However, some women choose to end breastfeeding because they go back to work (where it may be more difficult) or find they are exhausted. It takes a lot of calories and energy to breastfeed and sometimes your body will tell you it's had enough. If you can continue breastfeeding beyond a year, and it's working for you and your baby, then go for it!

Using Fingers and Utensils

Once your baby reaches this feeding stage, he will have a relatively well-developed pincer grasp and will be able to pick up small pieces of food in much the same manner that you would. Once your baby's pincer grasp is fully developed, he will pick up small items using the tip of his thumb and the side of his index finger. For most children, this is around 12 to 14 months of age. Once this occurs, your baby will be a faster and more confident eater.

At around 12 months of age, your child will begin to learn to scoop with a spoon. Up until now, it's been a lot of dipping. Dipping a spoon or stick of food into a soup, puree, or yogurt is the first step to learning how to self-feed with a spoon. Along with learning to scoop comes more mess, especially for the first few months. Your child will be about 16 to 18 months of age before she can rotate her wrist while keeping a spoon level and bringing it to her mouth. You can help your child learn these new scooping skills by having her high chair tray or tabletop at the right height. The longer the distance from the bowl to your baby's mouth, the more opportunity for the food to spill before it makes it to her mouth. Ideally, her elbows should be able to rest on the tabletop for support.

You'll also want to ensure that you have the right spoons for your child's needs. Different foods require different types of spoons. As baby's skills develop, you'll want to offer a spoon that matches his skill level. Some spoons are designed for parents to present the puree, such as the Gerber coated spoon. The handle is longer to accommodate an adult's grasp. The bowl of the spoon is flat and small, perfect for little mouths just learning to suck from the spoon. But for babies learning to dip, choose a tool designed just for that, like the NumNum dipper or pre-spoon. The handle is fat and short, so babies can grasp it easily. Too long of a handle and your child will have more difficulty rotating his wrist to place the dipper in his mouth. A flat dipper like this also allows little learners to "dip and flip" and not have to rotate the wrist at first, which is a more advanced skill.

The next step is a spoon with a slightly deeper bowl, as children learn to manage larger amounts of food in one mouthful and can engage their top lip to clean the deeper bowl with ease. Keep the handle short and fat or choose one like the Nuby, which has a wavy handle perfect for a smaller grasp.

The next step up is a slightly larger spoon-bowl, now that your toddler has a larger mouth. Now, your child can tolerate a harder metal spoon, but not too big! The spoons adults use are like shovels for their little mouths—keep it a manageable size, like the Gerber Kiddy Cutlery. It has a wider handle, a deeper bowl, and a slightly larger size for toddler mouths. Once your child has mastered this spoon, he may be ready for a regular spoon that adults use at the breakfast table for cereal or stirring their coffee. Remember, his open mouth needs to be as big as the "bowl" of the spoon.

Self Feeding with Spoons

- Early spoon choices may include the NumNum Dipper, Nuby, and Gerber Kiddy Cutlery, which have easy-to-grip handles and progressively larger spoon bowls (see photos of each on page 72).

- By 18 months, your child may be trying to scoop chunky noodle soup or cereal and milk. Try a kid's spoon that has holes in the spoon-bowl. It allows the extra liquid to drain out while keeping noodles or wet cereal on the spoon.

- A deeper spoon-bowl becomes easier for your child to manage because, over time, he has learned to rotate his wrist and turn the spoon-bowl into his open mouth without flipping the spoon upside down. That deeper spoon-bowl holds more food to be swallowed, and your child's larger mouth can now accommodate the bigger size.

Shortly after her first birthday, your child will also start to use a fork. With some hand-over-hand help, your child can learn to fork soft squares of non-slippery foods, such as cheese cubes. To help out, provide a barrier by putting a cheese cube in a large ice cube tray. This will help your child zero in on the food while bracing the fork against the sides of the tray.

Using a Straw

Continue to use straws as much as possible. Drinking from a straw can help build muscles in the face that help with chewing, swallowing, and speech development. Stay away from sippy cups. They encourage the tongue to move forward and back, rather than the upward motion needed to develop a mature swallow pattern (typically seen first around age one and fully mature by age two). This is a crucial time for this pattern to develop, and choosing the right cup (open or straw) is important. Keep the straw short, so that the tip of the straw just reaches the tip of the tongue, resting behind the lower teeth.

BY ABOUT 15 MONTHS OF AGE YOUR BABY SHOULD BE ABLE TO SPOON-FEED HERSELF 4 TO 6 OUNCES (112 TO 168 G) OF PUREE AT A MEAL WITH EASE, BUT IT STILL MIGHT BE A BIT MESSY.

Purees vs. Liquids

Purees are essentially thickened liquids. When a liquid is thickened, it is more manageable and easier to swallow. There is a smaller chance of aspiration (liquid or food entering the airway). It's a "learning food" that makes the process of swallowing easier and more comfortable at first.

Drinking from a Cup

You can also use an open cup at this time. In *Raising a Healthy, Happy Eater*, Melanie describes how to transition a toddler from a straw cup to an open cup. Begin by filling a short glass with water and adding a splash of juice, just to color the water. Spills will happen, so water is best—sugary juice is sticky when it spills. The small amount of juice is just to help your child see the surface of the water. Choose a short, clear glass container like an old baby food jar or small jelly jar. Wrap some rubber bands around the outside so little fingers get a better grip. Then, break the process into four separate steps, teaching each step and then chaining them together in a sequence:

1. Using hand-over-hand guidance, help your child lift the cup straight up from the table and set it back down. Practice several times, repeating the mantra, "Lift up, set down, stay dry."

2. Teach the second step by inserting a new step into the sequence noted in the first step above. The second step is to bring the threads to the lips, sip, but never tilt. Your toddler will be able to do this because he can see the surface of the water and it's filled high enough that there is no need to tip. If you opted out of using sippy cups, he will have practiced tipping and thus, pouring water down the front of his shirt. The mantra and sequence is now, "Lift up, cup to lips, sip, set down, stay dry." Practice this as many times as needed, replenishing the water level to ensure there is no need to tilt the cup.

3. Now that step 2 is mastered, you're ready to teach the tilt-up and, more important, if you want to avoid a spill, it's time to teach the tilt-down. Kids who spent months drinking from a sippy cup have trouble with this stage, because they are used to sipping and then pulling the cup away without immediately tipping it back down. To teach the tilt-down, say, "Put your cup on your tummy," as your child points to her entire chest and belly area. Kids seem to think that "tummy" means anything between shoulders and hips at this age. Now the mantra and sequence is as follows: "Lift up, cup to lips, sip, cup on your tummy." Repeat several times, but don't refill the glass. As the surface of the liquid lowers with each sip, the child will naturally tilt the glass slightly to sip. The key is the final step, "Put the cup on your tummy," which automatically causes the child to tilt the cup down.

4. Once your toddler has learned to put the edge of the cup on his tummy, he can either rest it there until getting another drink or follow through by then placing it back on the table.

Early Food Choices

At around 12 months of age your child is just beginning to express her opinion of things, but cognitively may still consider herself a part of her mommy or primary caregiver. By 18 months, she'll realize that she's a separate person from mommy, with separate (and often strong-willed) ideas. In terms of food, you need to set healthy guidelines for your child, and then guide her to make the right choices herself. If you let your child be in charge of what goes into her mouth she'll be fine, as long as the options provided are healthy. Don't make the choice between fish-shaped crackers and grapes. Make the choice between strawberries and grapes, both cut into safe-sized pieces.

One of the best things you can do to encourage your child to eat well is to consume healthy foods yourself. Children tend to want to eat what their parents eat. The first five years of life set up tastes and eating behaviors that will lay the foundation for your child's nutritional future. In the early years, children are greatly influenced by cultural and familial beliefs and attitudes surrounding food. Parents who model good eating habits in front of their children tend to have children who want to eat in a similar fashion.

Create a Stoplight Diet

Dr. Alison Ventura, an assistant professor at California Polytechnic State University, is an expert in self-regulation of food and studies how feeding experiences during early childhood affect the development of eating behaviors across the life span. She suggests creating a stoplight diet with the foods you eat. All foods get a color: green, yellow, or red. Green foods are foods you can eat all the time, such as fruits and vegetables; yellow foods are ones you can eat sometimes, such as cheese or pizza; and red foods are ones you should almost never eat, such as candy. Color-coding foods is a simple and easy way for kids to visualize which foods should play the most important roles in their diets.

Your Competent Eaters

- By one year of age your child should be eating three meals a day and one or two snacks.

- Your child now has increased trunk stability, greater chewing and swallowing skills, more teeth, a more developed pincer grasp, and the ability to start scooping up liquids with a spoon. As a result, she's a faster and more efficient eater.

- Continue to feed your child a mixture of soft handheld foods, safe finger foods, chopped foods, and purees. Although foods can be slightly harder, choking risks are still high at this age. You should avoid foods such as whole apples or stalks of celery, where large, hard chunks can come off.

- Your baby doesn't need formula after one year. However, there are continued benefits to receiving breast milk after a year. If you're still breastfeeding and it's working for you and your baby, continue to go for it!

- Your child will learn to scoop liquids with a spoon, rather than dip and lick the utensil. You can offer a spoon with a slightly bigger and deeper spoon-bowl to hold more liquids.

- Encourage drinking liquids using a cup or straw. Avoid sippy cups, as prolonged use may delay the development of a mature swallow pattern.

- Model healthy eating patterns for your child.

- Continue to offer a variety of healthy foods for your child, but don't become concerned if he won't eat something. Continue to offer the same food over time.

Veggie Frittata

Frittatas are a perfect consistency for kids to handle and they're packed with protein, healthy fats, and nutrients. For younger kids, chop the veggies into smaller pieces. Don't feel married to the veggies mentioned here. Feel free to experiment with what you have on hand.

1. Preheat the oven to 400°F (200°C, or gas mark 6).

2. In a medium bowl, beat together eggs, milk, flour, mustard, 1 tablespoon (15 ml) of the oil, and the salt. Let the batter stand for about 15 minutes.

3. Steam the carrots and asparagus for 3 to 5 minutes, or until tender.

4. Add the remaining 2 tablespoons (30 ml) oil to a 9-inch (23 cm) square baking dish. Heat in the oven for 10 minutes.

5. While the dish is warming, melt the butter in a large skillet over medium heat. Add the onion and garlic and cook until the onion starts to soften, about 3 minutes.

6. Add the green beans and cook for another 3 minutes. Add the tomatoes, cooked veggies, and basil and cook for another 2 or 3 minutes.

7. Carefully take the hot pan out of the oven and pour the batter evenly into the pan. Scatter the vegetable mixture on top. Bake for 30 minutes, or until puffed and lightly browned. Cut into squares and serve.

YIELD: 6 SERVINGS

2 eggs

¾ cup (180 ml) whole milk

¾ cup (90 g) all-purpose flour

2 tablespoons (22 g) whole-grain mustard

3 tablespoons (45 ml) olive oil, divided

⅛ teaspoon sea salt

2 carrots, chopped

5 asparagus stalks, chopped

2 tablespoons (28 g) butter

1 onion, chopped

2 cloves garlic, sliced

½ cup (50 g) chopped green beans

½ cup (75 g) chopped cherry tomatoes

1 tablespoon (3 g) finely chopped basil

Tofu and Tomato Curry

Many spices have wonderful health benefits. This mild curry recipe by Doctor Yum at DoctorYum.org is a delicious way to widen your child's taste palate and create a dish the whole family will love.

1. Heat the oil in a skillet over medium heat. Add the onion, ginger, and garlic and cook for about 3 minutes, or until the onions are soft.

2. Add the curry, turmeric, chili powder, and cinnamon and cook for another minute.

3. Add the tomatoes and reduce the heat to medium-low. Cook for 5 minutes, or until the tomatoes are soft.

4. Add the tofu and sugar and cook for another 5 minutes.

5. Add the coconut milk and bring the curry to a simmer. Remove the cinnamon stick and serve warm.

YIELD: 4 SERVINGS

2 tablespoons (30 ml) olive oil

1 onion, diced

1 slice ginger, minced

3 cloves garlic, minced

1 teaspoon curry powder

½ teaspoon turmeric

¼ teaspoon chili powder

1 cinnamon stick

5 tomatoes, diced

1 package (14 ounces, or 392 g) extra-firm tofu (freeze overnight and removed the next day to thaw)

2 tablespoons (25 g) sugar

1 cup (235 ml) coconut milk

Salt and pepper to taste

Health Benefits of Curry

Curry helps reduce inflammation, boost immunity, and increase the liver's ability to remove toxins from the body.

Roasted Chickpeas

Once your baby's pincer grasp improves she'll love picking up these roasted chickpeas. They're a high-protein snack that's chewy on the inside with a coating that's easy for your baby to feel in her mouth and slip down her throat. Be careful not to overcook chickpeas or they'll be too hard and no longer safe for your child.

1. Preheat the oven to 400°F (200°C, or gas mark 6). Line a baking sheet with parchment paper and set aside.

2. Spread the chickpeas on a paper towel and dab until dry.

3. Transfer the chickpeas to the prepared baking sheet and drizzle with the oil. Gently roll with a spoon until all the chickpeas are evenly coated. Sprinkle with the spices and roll again.

4. Roast the chickpeas for about 30 minutes, tossing them halfway through. Cool and serve.

YIELD: 4 SERVINGS

1 can (15 ounces, or 420 g) chickpeas, rinsed and drained

1 teaspoon olive oil

1 teaspoon onion powder

½ teaspoon garlic powder

½ teaspoon salt

Pint Size

You can feed these to younger babies by cutting the chickpeas in half.

Kid-Friendly Slow Cooker Chili

The slow cooker makes food so soft and tender that it's ideal for little mouths to eat. Plus, this chili is chunky enough for babies who are just learning to use a spoon.

1. Brown the ground beef in frying pan, then drain.

2. Place all the ingredients in a slow cooker and stir to combine.

3. Cook on high for 4 hours or on low for 8 hours.

4. Remove the bay leaf, cool, and serve.

YIELD: 10 SERVINGS

1 pound (454 g) ground beef

1 can (28 ounces, or 784 g) chopped tomatoes, with juice

1 can (15 ounces, or 420 g) tomato sauce

2 cans (15 ounces, or 420 g each) kidney beans, rinsed and drained

2 zucchini, diced into small cubes

2 red peppers, cored, seeded, and diced into small cubes

1 onion, diced into small cubes

2 cloves garlic, minced

1 teaspoon ground cumin

1 teaspoon chili powder

1 teaspoon (6 g) salt

1 bay leaf

Chili Balls

Combine cooked brown rice with leftover chili and form into 1-inch (2.5 cm) balls for a tasty finger food that all ages can enjoy.

Miso-Glazed Salmon Wraps

Fish oil is amazing for brain development, and we love to think of creative ways to get kids hooked on seafood from an early age. Chef Tonia Wilson created these wraps inspired by a California roll.

1. In a glass baking dish or zip-top bag, stir together the miso paste, soy sauce, honey, and hot water. Place the salmon in the marinade and let marinate for 1 to 4 hours in the refrigerator.

2. Cook the rice according to package directions and toss with 2 tablespoons (30 ml) of the rice wine vinegar and the vegetable oil. Let cool.

3. Toss the avocado with the remaining 1 tablespoon (15 ml) rice wine vinegar to prevent browning. Slice the nori into 1-inch (2.5 cm) strips, if using.

4. Heat the broiler on high. Remove the salmon from the marinade and place on a foil-lined baking sheet on the center rack and roast until just cooked through, about 12 minutes, depending on its thickness. Remove and allow the salmon to cool.

5. Pull the flesh apart into small pieces.

6. Assemble all the fillings (salmon, avocado, cucumber, green onion, rice, and nori) and place some of each ingredient in a piece of lettuce for the adults and older kids and in a bowl for younger children. Wrap and serve with sriracha, if desired.

YIELD: 4 SERVINGS

2 tablespoons (30 g) white miso paste (shiro style)

3 tablespoons (45 ml) soy sauce

1 tablespoon (20 g) honey

1 tablespoon (15 ml) hot water

1 pound (454 g) salmon fillet, deboned

1 cup (165 g) uncooked jasmine or other fragrant rice

3 tablespoons (45 ml) rice wine vinegar, divided

1 tablespoon (15 ml) vegetable oil

1 avocado, peeled, pitted, and diced

1 sheet nori (optional)

1 cup (120 g) finely diced English or mini cucumber

½ cup (50 g) finely sliced on diagonal green onion

1 head green or red leaf lettuce, leaves separated and washed

Sriracha or hot sauce (optional)

Monster Meatballs

Ground meat is moist and an easy protein for kids to chew, and meatballs will allow you to introduce some spices and new tastes.

1. Preheat the oven to 400°F (200°C, or gas mark 6). Spray a baking sheet with olive oil and set aside.

2. With your hands, mix all the ingredients together in a bowl. Once combined, roll the meat mixture into balls, approximately the size of a golf ball.

3. Spread out evenly on the pan and cook for about 20 minutes, or until cooked to an internal temperature of 165°F (74°C).

4. Serve the meatballs on their own with a side of veggies or with pasta and the tomato sauce recipe on page 168.

YIELD: 20 TO 24 MEATBALLS

Olive oil cooking spray

1 pound (454 g) ground beef

1 egg, beaten

½ cup (60 g) dry bread crumbs

⅓ cup (40 g) grated Parmesan cheese

½ onion, chopped

1 clove garlic, minced

¼ cup (12 g) chopped parsley

½ teaspoon dried oregano

¼ teaspoon salt

¼ teaspoon pepper

No Big Pieces

Panko bread crumbs are ideal for little kids.

Mini Savory Scones

Daniela Devitt, owner of YumBox.com, creates these mini treats. They're delightful as a dessert, but they're not too sweet. The scones are also the perfect size for little hands and a creative way to introduce new flavors and veggies to kids.

1. Preheat the oven to 375°F (190°C, or gas mark 5). Grease a mini muffin pan with butter.

2. In a large bowl, combine the oil, eggs, milk, and honey.

3. In a medium-size bowl combine the flour, baking powder, and salt. Add to the wet mixture and stir to combine.

4. Add the vegetables, cheese, and basil and blend again. The consistency will be a bit sticky.

5. Spoon the mixture into the mini muffin trays, filling just over halfway. Bake for about 18 minutes, or until golden brown.

YIELD: 24 MINI SCONES

Unsalted butter, for greasing pan

½ cup (120 ml) vegetable oil

2 eggs

¾ cup (180 ml) milk

1 to 2 tablespoons (15 to 30 ml) honey, to taste

2½ cups (300 g) all-purpose flour

2 teaspoons (8 g) baking powder

½ teaspoon salt

½ cup (75 g) diced red bell pepper

½ cup (35 g) chopped kale

½ cup (60 g) grated Pecorino cheese

¼ teaspoon ground basil

Be a Mix Master

You can blend any combination of vegetables and spices to use up what's in your fridge and introduce new tastes to your child. Some healthy options include fresh or dried herbs, raisins, sun-dried tomatoes, nuts, broccoli, shredded carrots, and raw spinach. If using zucchini or other wet vegetables, drain as much water as possible before adding. You can also experiment with cheese, trying feta, cheddar, Parmigiano-Reggiano, Pecorino, or just about any low-moisture cheese. For example, try broccoli, ham, and cheddar or spinach, olive, and feta.

Power Cookies

Let your baby's first experience with cookies be a healthy one. For kids who are always asking for chocolate chip cookies after dinner, try these power cookies as a satisfying and healthy treat.

1. Preheat the oven to 350°F (180°C, or gas mark 4). Line a baking sheet with parchment paper and set aside.

2. Combine the oats, chickpea flour, brown sugar, cinnamon, baking soda, and salt in a large bowl and set aside.

3. Combine the banana, coconut oil, vanilla, yogurt, chocolate chips, and walnuts, if using, in a separate bowl and pour into the dry ingredients, mixing until combined.

4. Use a spoon to scoop dough and form small (about 1-inch, or 2.5 cm) balls, placing them on the baking sheet.

5. Bake for 15 to 18 minutes, or until just brown on top.

YIELD: 24 COOKIES

2 cups (160 g) rolled oats

¾ cup (90 g) chickpea flour

⅔ cup (150 g) packed brown sugar

1 teaspoon ground cinnamon

½ teaspoon baking soda

¼ teaspoon salt

1 ripe banana, mashed

⅓ cup (80 ml) coconut oil, warmed and melted

1 teaspoon vanilla extract

¼ cup (60 g) Greek yogurt, plain or vanilla flavor

⅓ cup (60 g) chocolate chips

⅓ cup (45 g) walnuts, finely chopped (optional)

Nut-Free Option

Leave out the walnuts or replace with chopped sunflower or pumpkin seeds for a nut-free snack you can take anywhere.

REFERENCES

Alpha Galileo. "Coconut Oil Could Combat Tooth Decay." www.alphagalileo.org/ViewItem.aspx?ItemId=123571&CultureCode=en.

American Academy of Allergy Asthma & Immunology. "Increasing Rates of Allergies and Asthma." www.aaaai.org/conditions-and-treatments/library/allergy-library/prevalence-of-allergies-and-asthma.aspx.

———. "Interim Guidance on Early Peanut Introduction and Prevention of Peanut Allergy Published by JACI."

www.aaaai.org/about-the-aaaai/newsroom/news-releases/interim-guide-peanut.aspx.

American Academy of Pediatrics. "Mealtime TV Viewing During Pregnancy May Set Stage for Childhood Obesity." www.aap.org/en-us/about-the-aap/aap-press-room/pages/Mealtime-TV-Viewing-During-Pregnancy-May-Set-Stage-for-Childhood-Obesity.aspx.

———. "Policy Statement—Prevention of Choking Among Children." *Pediatrics* 125, no. 3 (2010): 601–607.

American Dietetic Association. "Vegetarian Diets Can Help Prevent Chronic Diseases." July 3, 2009.

American Heart Association. "Monounsaturated Fats." www.heart.org/HEARTORG/GettingHealthy/NutritionCenter/HealthyEating/Monounsaturated-Fats_UCM_301460_Article.jsp.

———. "Polyunsaturated Fats." www.heart.org/HEARTORG/GettingHealthy/NutritionCenter/HealthyEating/Polyunsaturated-Fats_UCM_301461_Article.jsp.

———. "Saturated Fats." www.heart.org/HEARTORG/GettingHealthy/NutritionCenter/HealthyEating/Saturated-Fats_UCM_301110_Article.jsp.

———. "Trans Fats." www.heart.org/HEARTORG/GettingHealthy/NutritionCenter/HealthyEating/Trans-Fats_UCM_301120_Article.jsp.

Anzman, S. L., et al. "Parental Influence on Children's Early Eating Environments and Obesity Risk: Implications for Prevention." *International Journal of Obesity* 34 (2010): 1116–1124.

Arvedson, J., and L. Brodsky. *Pediatric Swallowing and Feeding: Assessment and Management.* 2nd ed. New York: Singular Publishing Group, 2002.

Australian Capital Territory (ACT) Government. Kids at Play Fact Sheets. www.health.act.gov.au/healthy-living/kids-play.

Bentley, A. *Inventing Baby Food: Taste, Health, and the Industrialization of the American Diet.* Oakland, CA: University of California Press, 2014.

Berkey, C. S., et al. "Relation of Childhood Diet and Body Size to Menarche and Adolescent Growth in Girls." *American Journal of Epidemiology* 152, no. 5 (2000): 446–452.

Birch, L. L., L. Gunder, K. Grimm-Thomas, and D. G. Laing. "Infants' Consumption of a New Food Enhances Acceptance of Similar Foods." *Appetite* 30 (1998): 283–295.

Biro, F. M., et al. "Pubertal Assessment Method and Baseline Characteristics in a Mixed Longitudinal Study of Girls." *Pediatrics* 126, no. 3 (2010): e583–e590.

Bouchard, C. "Genetic Determinants of Regional Fat Distribution." *Human Reproduction* 12 (1997): 1–5.

Brown, A. "Differences in Eating Behavior, Well-Being and Personality Between Mothers Following Baby-Led vs. Traditional Weaning Styles." *Maternal and Child Nutrition* (2015).

Brown, A., and M. D. Lee. "Early Influences on Child Satiety-Responsiveness: The Role of Weaning Style." *Pediatric Obesity* 10, no. 1 (2015): 57–66.

———. "An Exploration of Experiences of Mothers Following a Baby-Led Weaning Style: Developmental Readiness for Complementary Foods." *Maternal & Child Nutrition* 9, no. 2 (2011): 233–243.

Brown, A., P. Raynor, and M. D. Lee. "Maternal Control of Child- Feeding During Breast and Formula Feeding in the First 6 Months Postpartum." *Journal of Human Nutrition and Dietetics* 24, no. 2 (2012): 177–186.

Byard, R. W., et al. "Safe Feeding Practices for Infants and Young Children." *Journal of Paediatrics and Child Health* 32, no. 4 (1996): 327–329.

Cameron, S. L., A. L. Heath, and R. W. Taylor. "Healthcare Professionals' and Mothers' Knowledge of, Attitudes to, and Experiences with, Baby-Led Weaning: A Content Analysis Study." *BMJ Open* 2, no. 6 (2012): e001542.

Cameron, S., et al. "How Feasible Is Baby-Led Weaning as an Approach to Infant Feeding? A Review of the Evidence." *Nutrients* 4, no. 11 (2012): 1575–1609.

Carruth, B. R., and J. D. Skinner. "Feeding Behaviors and Other Motor Development in Healthy Children (2–24 Months)." *Journal of the American College of Nutrition* 21 (2002): 88–96.

Carruth, B. R., P. Ziegler, A. Gordon, and S. I. Barr. "Prevalence of Picky Eaters among Infants and Toddlers and Their Caregiver's Decisions about Offering a Food." *Journal of the American Dietetic Association* 104 (2004): S57–S64.

Carruth, B. R., P. J. Ziegler, A. Gordon, and K. Hendricks. "Developmental Milestones and Self-Feeding Behaviors in Infants and Toddlers." *Journal of the American Dietetic Association* 104 (2004): s51–s56.

CASAColumbia. "The Importance of Family Dinners VIII." CASAColumbia White Paper, September 2012. www.casacolumbia.org/addiction-research/reports/importance-of-family-dinners-2012.

Cashdan, E., et al. "A Sensitive Period for Learning About Food." *Human Nature* 5, no. 3 (1994): 279–291.

Centers for Disease Control. "Trans Fat: The Facts." www.cdc.gov/nutrition/downloads/trans_fat_final.pdf.

Cesar, G. V., et al. "Association Between Breastfeeding and Intelligence, Educational Attainment, and Income at 30 Years of Age." *Lancet Global Health* 3, no. 4 (2015): e199–e205.

Christian, M. S., C. E. L. Evans, N. Hancock, C. Nykjaer, and J. E. Cade. "Family Meals

Can Help Children Reach Their 5 a Day: A Cross-Sectional Survey of Children's Dietary Intake from London Primary Schools." *Journal of Epidemiology & Community Health* 67, no. 4 (2013): 332–338.

Clavel-Chapelon, F. "Differential Effects of Reproductive Factors on the Risk of Pre- and Postmenopausal Breast Cancer: Results from a Large Cohort of French Women." *British Journal of Cancer* 86, no. 5 (2002): 723–727.

Clayton, H. B., et al. "Prevalence and Reasons for Introducing Infants Early to Solid Foods: Variations by Milk Feeding Type." *Pediatrics* 131, no. 4 (2013): e1108–e1114.

Committee on Obstetric Practice. "Committee Opinion No. 543: Timing of Umbilical Cord Clamping." *Obstetrics & Gynecology* 120, no. 6 (2012): 1522–1526.

Coulthard, H., G. Harris, and P. Emmett. "Delayed Introduction of Lumpy Foods to Children During the Complementary Feeding Period Affects Child's Food Acceptance and Feeding at 7 Years of Age." *Maternal & Child Nutrition* 5 (2009): 75–85.

Coulthard, M. "Distinguishing Between Salt Poisoning and Hypernatremic Dehydration in Children." *BMJ* 326, no. 7381 (2003): 157–160.

Crowe, F., et al. "Risk of Hospitalization or Death from Ischemic Heart Disease Among British Vegetarians and Nonvegetarians: Results from the EPIC-Oxford Cohort Study." *American Journal of Clinical Nutrition* 97 (2013): 597–603.

Department of Health, New York State. "Choking Prevention for Children." www.health.ny.gov/prevention/injury_prevention/choking_prevention_for_children.htm.

Devaney, B., P. Ziegler, S. Pac, V. Karwe, and S. I. Barr. "Nutrient Intakes of Infants and Toddlers." *Journal of the American Dietetic Association* 104 (2004): S14–S21.

Dietitians of Canada. "Food Sources of Vitamin C." www.dietitians.ca/Your-Health/Nutrition-A-Z/Vitamins/Food-Sources-of-Vitamin-C.aspx.

Du Toit, G., et al. "Randomized Trial of Peanut Consumption in Infants at Risk for Peanut Allergy." The New England Journal of Medicine 372 (2015): 803–813.

Dube, K., J. Schwartz, M. J. Mueller, H. Kalhoff, and M. Kersting. "Iron Intake and Iron Status in Breastfed Infants During the First Year of Life." *Clinical Nutrition* 29 (2010): 773–778.

Ervin, R. B., et al. "Consumption of Added Sugar Among US Children and Adolescents, 2005–2008." NCHS Data Brief No. 87, 2012.

European Food Information Council. "Child and Adolescent Nutrition." www.eufic.org/article/en/page/BARCHIVE/expid/basics-child-adolescent-nutrition.

———. "Omega-3 Fatty Acids: Where to Find Them?" www.eufic.org/article/en/artid/omega-3-fatty-acids.

Fernando, N., and M. Potock. *Raising a Healthy, Happy Eater: A Parent's Handbook: A Stage-by-Stage Guide to Setting Your Child on the Path to Adventurous Eating*. New York: The experiment, 2015, 117–118.

Fewtrell, M. "Six Months of Exclusive Breastfeeding: How Good Is the Evidence?" *BMJ* 342 (2011).

Fisher, J. O., D. C. Mitchell, H. Smiciklas-Wright, and L. L. Birch. "Parental Influences on Young Girls' Fruit and Vegetable, Micronutrient, and Fat Intakes." *Journal of the American Dietetic Association* 102 (2002): 58–64.

Food Allergy Research & Education. "Facts and Statistics." www.foodallergy.org/facts-and-stats.

Fowler, S., et al. "Fueling the Obesity Epidemic? Artificially Sweetened Beverage Use and Long-Term Weight Gain." *Obesity* 16, no. 8 (2008): 1894–1900.

Gao, X., et al. "Meeting Adequate Intake for Dietary Calcium without Dairy Foods in Adolescents Aged 9 to 18." *Journal of the American Dietetic Association* 106, no. 11 (2006): 1759–1765.

Gatto, K. K. Understanding the Orofacial Complex: Muscle Manual. Denver, CO: Outskirts Press, 2014.

Government of Canada. "Infant Feeding." www.hc-sc.gc.ca/fn-an/nutrition/infant-nourisson/index-eng.php.

Gurr, M. I. "The Consequences of Early Over Nutrition for Fall Cell Size and Number: The Pig as an Experimental Model for Human Obesity." *International Journal of Obesity* 1, no. 2 (1977): 151–170.

Harris, C. S., S. P. Baker, G. A. Smith, and R. M. Harris. "Childhood Asphyxiation by Food: A National Analysis and Overview." *JAMA* 251, no. 17 (1984): 2231–2235.

Hauser, G. J., D. Chitayat, L. Berns, D. Braver, and B. Muhlbauer. "Peculiar Odours in Newborns and Maternal Prenatal Ingestion of Spicy Foods." *European Journal of Pediatrics* 144, no. 4 (1985): 403.

Hausner, H., W. L. P. Bredie, C. Mølgaard, M. A. Petersen, and P. Møller. "Differential Transfer of Dietary Flavour Compounds into Human Breast Milk." *Physiology & Behavior* 95, no. 1–2 (2008): 118–124.

Healthy Child. "Fats and Oils for Children's Health." www.healthychild.com/fats-and-oils-for-childrens-health.

Hetherington, M. M. "A Step-by-Step Introduction to Vegetables at the Beginning of Complementary Feeding. The Effects of Early and Repeated Exposure." *Appetite* 84 (2015): 280–290.

Illi, S., et al. "Protection from Childhood Asthma and Allergy in Alpine Farm Environments: The GABRIEL Advanced Studies." *The Journal of Allergy and Clinical Immunology* 129, no. 6 (2012): 1470–1477.

Institute of Medicine. "Dietary Reference Intakes for Calcium and Vitamin D." Report brief. April 21, 2012.

———. "Dietary Reference Intakes for Energy, Carbohydrate, Fiber, Fat, Fatty Acids, Cholesterol, Protein, and Amino Acids." http://iom.nationalacademies.org/reports/2002/dietary-reference-intakes-for-energy-carbohydrate-fiber-fat-fatty-acids-cholesterol-protein-and-amino-acids.aspx#sthash.qPzXOjh8.dpuf.

International Foundation for Functional Gastrointestinal Disorders. "Kids and Dietary Fiber." www.aboutkidsgi.org/site/treatments/kids-and-dietary-fiber.

Karimi, M., et al. "Acetaminophen Use and the Symptoms of Asthma, Allergic Rhinitis and Eczema in Children." *Iranian Journal of Allergy, Asthma, and Immunology* 5, no. 2 (2006): 63–67.

Kostyak, J. C., et al. "Relative Fat Oxidation Is Higher in Children Than Adults." *Nutrition Journal* 6 (2007): 19.

Lewis, D. S., H. A. Bartrand, C. A. McMahan, H. C. McGill, K. D. Carey, and E. J. Masoro. "Preweaning Food Intake Influences the Adiposity of Young Adult Baboons." *Journal of Clinical Investigation* 78 (1986): 899–905.

Lucas, A. "Long-Term Programming Effects of Early Nutrition: Implications for the Preterm Infant." *Journal of Perinatology* 25 (2005): S2–S6.

———. "Programming by Early Nutrition: An Experimental Approach." *Journal of Nutrition* 128, no. 2 (1998): 401S–406S.

Lukasewycz, L. D., and J. A. Mennella. "Lingual Tactile Acuity and Food Texture Preference in Children and Their Mothers." *Food Quality and Preference* 26 (2012): 58–66.

Mangels, R. "Iron in the Vegan Diet." The Vegetarian Resource Group. www.vrg.org/nutrition/iron.php.

Mayo Clinic. "Does My Baby Need a Vitamin D Supplement?" www.mayoclinic.org/healthy-lifestyle/infant-and-toddler-health/expert-answers/vitamin-d-for-babies/faq-20058161.

———. "Infant and Toddler Health." www.mayoclinic.org/healthy-lifestyle/infant-and-toddler-health/expert-answers/vitamin-d-for-babies/faq-20058161.

———. "Iron Deficiency Anemia." www.mayoclinic.org/diseases-conditions/iron-deficiency-anemia/basics/prevention/con-20019327.

———. "Iron Deficiency in Children: Tips for Parents." www.mayoclinic.org/healthy-lifestyle/childrens-health/in-depth/iron-deficiency/art-20045634.

———. "Trans Fat Is Double Trouble for Your Heart Health." www.mayoclinic.org/diseases-conditions/high-blood-cholesterol/in-depth/trans-fat/art-20046114.

McCance, R. A. "Food Growth and Time." *Lancet* 2 (1962): 271–272.

Mennella J. A., A. Johnson, and G. K. Beauchamp. "Garlic Ingestion by Pregnant Women Alters the Odor of Amniotic Fluid." Chemical Senses 20, no. 2 (1995): 207–209.

Mennella, J. A., L. D. Lukasewycz, S. M. Castor, and G. K. Beauchamp. "The Timing and Duration of a Sensitive Period in Human Flavor Learning: A Randomized Trial." *American Journal of Clinical Nutrition* 93 (2011): 1019–1024.

Mennella, J. A., L. D. Lukasewycz, J. W. Griffith, and G. K. Beauchamp. "Evaluation of a Forced-Choice, Paired-Comparison Tracking Procedure Method for Determining Taste Preferences Across the Lifespan." *Chemical Senses* 36 (2011): 345–355.

Mennella, J. A., J. Trabulsi, and L. Inamdar. "The Sensory World of Formula-Fed Infants: Differences Among Artificial Milk Feedings in Flavor Learning and Satiety." In *Dietary and Nutritional Aspects of Bottle Feeding*, edited by V. R. Preedy. Wageningen, The Netherlands: Wageningen Academic Publishers, 95–116.

Mennella, J. A., et al. "Experience in Mother's Milk Modifies the Infant's Acceptance of Flavored Cereal." *Developmental Psychobiology* 35, no. 3 (1999): 197–203.

Mennella, J. A., et al. "Preferences for Salty and Sweet Tastes Are Elevated and Related to Each Other during Childhood." *PLOS One* 3 (2014): e92201.

Mennella, J. A., et al. *"Prenatal and Postnatal Flavor Learning by Human Infants."* Pediatrics 107, no. 6 (2001): E88.

Montgomery, P., et al. "Low Blood Long Chain Omega-3 Fatty Acids in UK Children Are Associated with Poor Cognitive Performance and Behavior: A Cross-Sectional Analysis from the DOLAB Study." *PLoS One* 8, no. 6 (2013).

Morris, S. "A Profile of the Development of Oral-Motor Skills in Early Infancy—Birth to 12 Months." Unpublished work, 1991.

Moshfegh, A. J., J. Goldman, and L. Cleveland. *What We Eat in America, NHANES 2005–2006: Usual Nutrient Intakes from Food and Water Compared to 1997 Dietary Reference Intakes for Vitamin D, Calcium, Phosphorus, and Magnesium*. Washington, DC: U.S. Department of Agriculture, Agricultural Research Service, 2012.

Namath, A. "Restaurant Highchairs Dirtier Than Toilet Seats?" *Food Safety News*, October 15, 2010. www.foodsafetynews.com/2010/10/study-high-chairs-contain-more-bacteria-than-toilet-seats/#.VoMqU8r1FGc.

National Health Service (UK). "Your Baby's First Solid Foods." www.nhs.uk/Conditions/pregnancy-and-baby/Pages/solid-foods-weaning.aspx#close.

National Obesity Observatory. "Determinants of Obesity: Child Diet." October 2012. www.noo.org.uk/securefiles/151230_0122//Child-dietfactsheetDec2015.pdf.

Naylor, A., and A. Morrow. *Developmental Readiness of Normal Full-Term Infants to Progress from Exclusive Breastfeeding to the Introduction of Complementary Foods: Reviews of the Relevant Literature Concerning Infant Immunologic, Gastrointestinal, Oral Motor and Maternal Reproductive and Lactational Development*. Washington, DC: Academy for Educational Development, 2001.

Newman, J., and A. Taylor. "Effect of a Means-End Contingency on Young Children's Food Preferences." *Journal of Experimental Child Psychology* 53, no. 2 (1992): 200–216.

Northstone, K., P. Emmett, and F. Nethersole. "The Effect of Age of Introduction to Lumpy Solids on Foods Eaten and Reported Feeding Difficulties at 6 and 15 Months." *Journal of Human Nutrition and Dietetics* 14 (2001): 43–54.

Nutri-Facts. "Essential Fatty Acids." www.nutri-facts.org/eng/essential-fatty-acids/essential-fatty-acids/intake-recommendations.

O'Connell, J. M., et al. "Growth of Vegetarian Children: The Farm Study." *Pediatrics* 84, no. 3 (1989): 475–481.

Pepino, M. Y., and J. A. Mennella. "Factors Contributing to Individual Differences in Sucrose Preference." *Chemical Senses* 30 (2005): i319–i320.

Physicians Committee for Responsible Medicine. "Vegetarian Diets for Children: Right from the Start." www.pcrm.org/health/diets/vegdiets/vegetarian-diets-for-children-right-from-the-start.

Potock, M. *Happy Mealtimes with Happy Kids: How to Teach Your Child about the Joy of Food!* Raleigh, NC: Lulu, 2014.

Pridham, K. F. "Feeding Behavior of 6- to 12-Month-Old Infants: Assessment and Sources of Parental Information." *Journal of Pediatrics* 117 (1990): S174–S180.

Raising Children Network. "Good Fats and Bad Fats: The Basics." www.raisingchildren.net.au/articles/fat_basics.html.

Rapley, G. "Baby-Led Weaning: Transitioning to Solid Foods at the Baby's Own Pace." *Community Practitioner* 84 (2011): 20–23.

Renfrew, M. J., S. Pokhrel, and M. Quigley. *Preventing Disease and Saving Resources: The Potential Contribution of Increasing Breastfeeding Rates in the UK.* London: UNICEF, 2012.

Rheingold, H. "Development as the Acquisition of Familiarity." *Annual Review of Psychology* 36 (1985): 1–18.

Rizzo, N. S., J. Sabate, K. Jaceldo-Siegl, and G. E. Fraser. "Vegetarian Dietary Patterns Are Associated with a Lower Risk of Metabolic Syndrome: The Adventist Health Study 2." *Diabetes Care* 34, no. 5 (2011): 1225–1227.

Roper, H. P., and T. J. David. "Decline in Deaths from Choking on Food in Infancy: An Association with Change in Feeding Practice?" *Journal of the Royal Society of Medicine* 80, no. 1 (1987): 2–3.

Savage, J. S., et al. "Parental Influence on Eating Behavior." *Journal of Law, Medicine & Ethics* 35, no. 1 (2007): 22–34.

Schaal, B., L. Marlier, and R. Soussignan. "Human Foetuses Learn Odours from Their Pregnant Mother's Diet." *Chemical Senses* 25 (2000): 729–737.

Scheibye-Knudsen, M., et al. "A High-Fat Diet and NAD Activate Sirt1 to Rescue Premature Aging in Cockayne Syndrome." *Cell Metabolism* 20, no. 5 (2014): 840.

Schwartz, C., J. Madrelle, C. M. J. L. Vereijken, H. Weenen, S. Nicklaus, and M. M. Hetherington. "Complementary Feeding and *'Donner les Bases du Goût'* (Providing the Foundation of Taste). A Qualitative Approach to Understand Weaning Practices, Attitudes and Experiences by French Mothers." *Appetite* 71 (2013): 321–331.

Searing, D. A., and D. Y. M. Leung. "Vitamin D in Atopic Dermatitis, Asthma and Allergic Diseases." *Immunology and Allergy Clinics of North America* 30, no. 3 (2010): 397–409.

Simopoulos, A. P. "The Importance of the Ratio of Omega-6/Omega-3 Essential Fatty Acids." *Biomedicine & Pharmacotherapy* 56, no. 8 (2002): 365–379.

Steer, C. D., et al. "The Variation in Stool Patterns from 1 to 42 Months: A Population-Based Observational Study." *Archives of Disease in Childhood* 94, no. 3 (2009): 231–233.

SymphonyIRI Group. The Food Institute: Millennial Shoppers: Tapping into the Next Growth Segment. https://foodinstitute.com/images/media/iri/TTJune2012.pdf.

———. Pulse Report Baby. www.iriworldwide.com/IRI/media/IRI-Clients/PulseReport_Baby_Q2-14_Final.pdf.

Townsend, E. "Baby Knows Best? The Impact of Weaning Style on Food Preferences and Body Mass Index in Early Childhood in a Case-Controlled Sample." *BMJ* 2 (2012): e000298.

Trabulsi, J. C., and J. A. Mennella. "Diet, Sensitive Periods in Flavour Learning, and Growth." *International Review of Psychiatry* 24, no. 3 (2012): 219–230.

University of Minnesota. "Turn Off the TV During Family Meals." *ScienceDaily*, October 2007. www.sciencedaily.com/releases/2007/10/071014200545.htm.

US Food and Drug Administration. "Foodborne Illness & Contaminants." www.fda.gov/Food/FoodborneIllnessContaminants.

USDA. "SuperTracker." www.cdc.gov/nutrition/everyone/basics/fat/index.html?s_cid=tw_ob294.

USDA Agricultural Research Service. "Sodium Intake Reassessed for 2007–2008: Result of Discontinuation of Data Processing Step on Salt Adjustment, Mean Amounts Consumed per Individual, in the United States, 2007–2008 and 2009–2010." December 16, 2013.

Vangay, P., et al. "Antibiotics, Pediatric Dysbiosis, and Disease." *Cell Host & Microbe* 17, no. 5 (2015): 553–564.

Vegetarian Nutrition. "Vegetarian Nutrition for School-Aged Children." http://vegetariannutrition.net/docs/School-Aged-Children-Vegetarian-Nutrition.pdf.

Vegetarian Resource Group. "How Many Teens and Other Youth Are Vegetarian and Vegan? The Vegetarian Resource Group Asks in a 2014 National Poll." May 30, 2014. www.vrg.org/blog/2014/05/30/how-many-teens-and-other-youth-are-vegetarian-and-vegan-the-vegetarian-resource-group-asks-in-a-2014-national-poll.

Ventura, A., L. Inamdar, and J. A. Mennella. "A Model System to Understand Satiation and Self-Regulation of Intake During Infancy." *Pediatric Obesity* 10, no. 3 (2014): 180–187.

Washington University in St. Louis. "Parents Shape Whether Their Children Learn to Eat Fruits and Vegetables." *ScienceDaily*, August 2008. www.sciencedaily.com/releases/2008/08/080811200425.htm.

World Health Organization. *Sugars Intake for Adults and Children.* Geneva: WHO, 2015.

Zajonc, R. "Attitudinal Effects of Mere Exposure." *Journal of Personality and Social Psychology* 9, no. 2, pt. 2 (1968): 1.

Acknowledgments

We'd like to thank Jessica Haberman and the wonderful team at Quarto Publishing Group for encouraging us to create the book we wish we'd had when our own children were first introduced to solids. We hope that this book will give you the courage to experiment with different tastes and textures in your children's meals from an early age. Know that your child needn't live on a diet of bland, mushy foods in order to be safe—in fact, the opposite is true.

We'd also love to thank all of the insightful and talented experts who have offered their time and advice in the making of this book. Specifically, Dr. Jack Newman, who has arguably done more for women and breastfeeding than anyone else around. His passion for the early nutrition of children is inspiring.

We're also extremely thankful to Alison Ventura for sharing her extensive research and insights into the world for of self-feeding. Our gratitude extends to the nationally renowned feeding experts who provided their insights, including Diane Bahr, Marsha Dunn Klein, Marjorie Meyer Palmer, and Catherine Shaker. Thank you, too, to all the moms, chefs, doctors, and pint-sized testers who helped us with our recipes.

Lastly, we are so thankful to the love and support of our families, who rooted us on as we typed madly and spent hours on the phone with one author in Colorado and the other in Canada. Thank you for continuing to smile and love us, even when we didn't have time to make dinner because we were busy writing about *other* people making dinner.

About the Authors

Nancy Ripton is a writer and editor with two decades of experience in consumer publishing. She has written for numerous international publications including: *Pregnancy, Fit Pregnancy, Today's Parent, Self, More, Elle, Glamour, Men's Fitness,* and *Chatelaine.* In her pre-baby life, she was the editor-in-chief of *Oxygen* and *glow* magazines, and she recently returned to the workforce full-time at the helm of *Inside Fitness Women.*

With a background as a personal trainer and fitness program director, Nancy has always been passionate about health, fitness, nutrition, and learning new ways to strive towards optimal health. When she had children, her desire to learn about nutrition expanded into researching healthy ways to get kids to eat better in today's sugar-laden society.

Nancy, a mother of three, is also a popular parenting blogger. She co-founded JustTheFactsBaby.com after having her first child nine years ago, and it has grown to be a go-to site for parents to find trusted, well-researched parenting advice. This is her first book.

Melanie Potock, M.A., CCC-SLP, is an international speaker, a pediatric feeding specialist, and certified speech-language pathologist. Her practice focuses on the family and teaching the fundamentals of parenting in the kitchen.

Melanie has over 15 years of experience helping babies, children, and teens learn to eat a variety of healthy foods. The spectrum of kids on her caseload includes children with significant medical issues to the garden-variety picky eater.

Her extensive knowledge of how children learn the developmental process known as "feeding" and her joyful approach in supporting the whole family on their feeding journey are the perfect combination for leading families toward happier, healthier mealtimes for everyone.

She is the coauthor of *Raising a Healthy, Happy Eater* and author of *Happy Mealtimes with Happy Kids.*

INDEX